T0300819

You Can't Say That Any More

You Can't Say That Any More

Prof. Ivor Vertue
with Bruno Vincent

abacus
books

ABACUS

First published in Great Britain in 2024 by Abacus

1 3 5 7 9 10 8 6 4 2

A CIP catalogue record for this book
is available from the British Library.

ISBN 978-0-349-14666-9

Typeset in Garamond by M Rules
Printed and bound in Great Britain by
Clays Ltd, Elcograf S.p.A.

Papers used by Abacus are from well-managed forests
and other responsible sources.

Abacus
An imprint of
Little, Brown Book Group
Carmelite House
50 Victoria Embankment
London EC4Y 0DZ

An Hachette UK Company
www.hachette.co.uk

www.littlebrown.co.uk

A Note to the Reader

It is now widely accepted (I would say 'a truth universally acknowledged', if it was at all safe in this day and age to approve of the highly problematic Jane Austen) that the modern reader needs to be protected from the harmful attitudes of the past.

When looking at supposedly 'classic' movies and TV, 'great' literature and 'innocent' children's entertainment, we are assailed from every side by appalling values. In *Titus Andronicus*, for instance, the title character tricks a woman into eating a pie made from the flesh of her own sons. It is almost as though Shakespeare is deliberately goading us. Has he no respect for those with gluten intolerance or coeliac disease? Does he not care for the feelings of vegetarians or vegans? Is he taking a racist–colonialist potshot at the cannibalistic tribes still dwelling in Papua New Guinea, who have no way of defending themselves (except, of course, by eating their enemies)?

Chaucer has been hailed as the first great writer in English. Yet could anything more emphatically reinforce the inequities of the North–South divide (with its accompanying gap in wealth and opportunities) than writing about a pilgrimage to

Canterbury of all places, deep within the bosom of the complacently wealthy south-east? If he had an ounce of respect for the concept of 'levelling up', would he not have sent his pilgrims to Skegness, Skelmersdale or Scunthorpe?

Even popular texts for *children* are not safe from this scourge. After all, can we really allow a character to be called Winnie the Pooh? Are we not endangering the young with lifelong complexes about faeces, possibly encouraging generations obsessed with scatology and even coprophagia? (To me, the answer seems so simple: change the name to Lucy the Wee! Let us not foster the acquisition of dung, but encourage the release of urine!)

Previous generations have shown their own complicity with these systems of oppression by turning a blind eye. This will not stand!

I have taken upon myself the task of expunging the harmful messages and offensive tropes which abound everywhere you look within the world of literature, television and cinema. I offer only humble suggestions, which I have striven to ensure are *strictly* in line with the most progressive standards of our society. At least, as much as possible: if some of my phraseology has aged badly in the weeks between final manuscript and publication, as seems entirely plausible, I expect to be thoroughly chastised and shunned by many of my contemporaries.

Finally, to those who baulk at my suggestions, be assured I am not trying to cancel culture, only to provide it with a safe and comfortable rail-replacement bus service.

PROF. IVOR VERTUE,
Folkestone Wetherspoons, April 2024

About Prof. Ivor Vertue

Ivor Vertue completed a PhD in the depiction of sticky-back plastic in 1980s children's television from the University of Bexhill, and is a co-host (with the TikTok wild-knitting sensation Persephone Toynboyle) of the podcast *Mullet Over* – an unashamedly geeky episode-by-episode re-evaluation of Pat Sharp's *Fun House*. A well-known face on the Sidcup poetry slam scene, he also placed third in the all-Kent pole-dance-a-palooza in 2021.

Contents

Romeo and Juliet
by William Shakespeare

Shakespeare's great romantic tragedy, probably first performed in 1597, follows the story of two teenage 'star-cross'd lovers' who meet a tragic end. Their families, the Montagues and the Capulets, are competing factions in a 'turf war', a vicious and unstoppable blood feud memorably put to music in the theme tune to *The Apprentice*. Despite (or perhaps partly because of) overt disapproval and threats from family members and authority figures, Romeo and Juliet fall in love.

The plot can be understood by modern readers as a 'pre-make' of Steven Spielberg's *West Side Story* – a canny marketing move on Shakespeare's part. However, the story features (and may be seen to encourage) multiple instances of extremely dangerous themes for modern readers: drug use; accidental overdoses; teenage knife crime; unprotected sex; unsafe and unsupervised balcony usage; and an outdated and sexist depiction of a female nurse as a protective maternal figure, which can be offensive to nurses who may feel judged by not fitting this criterion.

Potential trigger warnings

! Authority defiance disorder
! Peer pressure
! Gang violence
! Lack of adequate sex education/risk of unexpected teenage pregnancy
! Citizens of Verona may well be offended or emotionally damaged by its depiction as a crime-ridden city, when in fact crime rates are currently among the lowest in the region and the city has multiple positive reviews on both Tripadvisor and Google Maps

Problematic quotations

'A plague o' both your houses': triggering for sufferers of long Covid and upsetting for people with no fixed abode.

'That which we call a rose,/By any other word would smell as sweet': stigmatises those with no sense of smell and seems to mock those allergic to the scent of roses.

'Romeo, Romeo, wherefore art thou, Romeo?': overly ornate language incomprehensible to modern audiences. Suggest Juliet texting her lover: 'Romeo where tf r u? 🏛'.

Suggested revisions

The apothecary is directly responsible for the death of the two main characters. This stigmatises non-traditional and homeopathic medicine, its users and practitioners. Suggest changing the apothecary to a representative of Big Pharma, selling opioids. Also, his lack of adequate safety instructions for the use of his products could stoke fear of *mainstream* medical practitioners and cause symptoms of diseases to go untreated. The Montagues and Capulets should form a class action lawsuit against him.

Offensively heteronormative choice of character names: suggest androgynous replacements such as Sam and Kim, or Tom/Thom and Gerry/Jerri.

The ending in which both Romeo and Juliet die will be very emotionally damaging for modern readers. Both of them should survive and commit to a long-term relationship, couples' therapy and a visit to a family planning clinic.

The Wind in the Willows by Kenneth Grahame

Kenneth Grahame's charming book about the exploits of Mole, Ratty, Badger and Toad is a picture of apparently financially stable upper-middle-class cis-males enjoying large amounts of leisure time in the untouched English countryside. It will be alienating for young readers on many levels, primarily because they cannot relate to the lifestyle, and have ahead of them a life of wage-slavery and retirement probably in their late seventies.

The exquisite rural picturesqueness is a vision of a world gone by, and ought to be rewritten showing large amounts of litter and fly-tipping in the woods, the roads at a standstill with queues of lorries going back to Dover, and the characters all being suspicious and distrustful of each other's motives, with natural habitats ravaged by intensive farming methods and harmful pesticides.

Problematic quotations

'Believe me, my young friend, there is nothing – absolutely nothing – half so much worth doing as simply messing about in boats': messing about is strictly to be discouraged in boats, as it is extremely dangerous. Under current legislation, all passengers must familiarise themselves with (and preferably memorise) safety procedures, including the locations of life-jackets, first-aid kits, fire extinguishers, flares, rubber dinghies, air pumps, whistles and safe exit points.

Suggested revisions

It is entirely inappropriate for Ratty, Mole and Toad to go off in something referred to as a 'gypsy caravan'. The phrasing is outdated (a 'traditional Romany or Traveller vardo' might be acceptable) but more importantly it is cultural appropriation – just as they oughtn't to spend a weekend renting out an igloo or wigwam (although an internet search reveals that sadly such inappropriate experiences are widely available and popular) – they should instead be driving a white transit van.

Toad's obsession with a motor car is perhaps understandable for a piece of fiction written at the dawn of the internal combustion engine, when roads were empty and before the invention of leaded petrol. However, now it strikes the wrong note. Recommend he falls in love with his new Tesla, which he crashes owing to the extreme acceleration capabilities, albeit he ought to drop some warning remarks about the company owner's disturbing obsession with 'absolute free speech'.

The spectacle of Toad (a cis-male) dressed in female clothes (of a working-class washerwoman), escaping prison and then driving dangerously is a deeply troubling portrayal of a trans-spectrum character, which amounts to hate speech – this passage is irredeemable and must be cut out.

The Flintstones
(Hanna-Barbera)

The depiction of the ordinary American family as a clan of Stone Age cave dwellers has aged well as a satirical device, especially considering the pre-Civil Rights American era in which the Hanna-Barbera series was made, and the anti-democratic and liberal-hostile agenda which has taken sway among grassroots traditional America.

But instead of the savage (pun intended) take-down of picket-fence values one might expect, the family is depicted as a haven of domestic security and viewed with warm indulgence rather than the jaw-dropping horror that would be more appropriate.

Potential trigger warnings

! Domestic animal abuse (kicking the cat out through
  the front door in the closing credits)

! The wearing of animal fur depicted as common and acceptable – change to faux fur

Problematic quotations

'Yabba dabba doo!': Fred's yells of jubilation (as well as his frequent screams of dismay) are a display of his poor emotional regulation and create a potentially disturbing domestic atmosphere for his children. He should instead just nod calmly and take things in his stride, seeking not to overreact in order to set a better example.

'Gonna have a gay old time': despite this apparent gesture towards LGBTQIA+ inclusivity, there is a staunch refusal to acknowledge anything other than thriving heteronormativity even here during the Stone Age – an era of supposed bestial lawlessness. It would be more appropriate for Fred and Barney to be having a torrid sexual affair in a hidden cave.

Suggested revisions

The show is a veritable smorgasbord of historical inaccuracy liable to lace any young viewer's mind with confusion and incorrect information. Dinosaurs, in particular, were not contemporaneous with Stone Age people; nor was leaving a stone bottle outside a residence likely to result in it being filled with milk the following morning. Such flights of fancy may lead to a rose-tinted view of early humans and their struggles against a merciless universe.

In the credits, the Flintstones and the Rubbles are depicted going to watch a movie and then going to a drive-thru. This relaxing leisure activity is a non-realistic view of the daily struggles of life at the dawn of human civilisation. It would be preferable for them to be shown performing realistic activities – scavenging from the carcass of a dead bison or engaging in bloody tit-for-tat tribal warfare.

The show features a kangaroo, which has never been native to North America (the presumed setting for the series, albeit this is not made explicit). In fact, Caucasian Stone Age man did not populate either the North American or the Australian land masses – the earliest human settlers being the Native Americans and First Nations of Australia. To be acceptable, the show should be reproduced from scratch to reflect these important differences, or else justly be accused of adding *fictional* continental colonialism on top of the crimes of its factual counterpart.

It is not promoting safety to show a family keeping a sabre-tooth tiger as a pet. Instead, in the opening credits, they should stalk and kill it, then eat its flesh for dinner.

Running while carrying the weight of a log-frame stone-wheel car is liable to cause serious lumbar and muscular distress and must be strenuously discouraged – for Fred's journey to work he should walk.

Bamm-Bamm – Barney and Betty's son – is a preternaturally strong and violent toddler who can only say 'bam bam', and smash things. This promotes harmful generalisations about male youth violence. Change his name to something more positive and healthy but equally adaptable to the infant tongue, such as 'Cous Cous'.

'Bedrock', their home town, has suspicious and

potentially subversive sexual connotations indicating marital activity. Change to something more innocent sounding, like 'Mudpassage' or 'Fertile Valley Entrance'.

Where's Wally?
by Martin Handford

Time and time again when picking up a beloved old text which appears to be the picture of innocence, you take one look and think at once, 'Wow, why didn't someone see this before?'

For no book could this be more true than the internationally bestselling *Where's Wally? / Where's Waldo?* brand, which has been on bookshelves in almost every home and library since the late-1980s.

Most books aimed at children understandably have a child as the main character. Here is a whole series where the protagonist is a solo adult man who never speaks to anyone, has no friends, interacts with no one, yet can always be found at the back of large bustling crowds trying not to draw attention to himself. His motives are inscrutable, his disguise (that of an effete football enthusiast) unconvincing. If one considers what he might *actually* be up to, his expression of studied innocence becomes frankly sinister. On top of this there is his continuous and restless roaming among tourist attractions,

11

holiday parks, airports, beaches and funfairs. One's blood runs cold when speculating as to what it is he is waiting for a chance to do.

Naïve art students could claim Handford's art style is in the *Wimmelbilderbuch* tradition, which builds on work by Hieronymus Bosch and Pieter Bruegel the Elder. Those two artists sometimes composed panoramas of horror peopled by monsters, violence, pestilence and death – yet in its antiseptic plainness, containing its one elusive red spot, Wally's world is somehow more terrifying.

Suggested revisions

To reverse the sinister alienation of the extant artworks, Wally should be depicted clearly in the centre, hanging out with a diverse group of friends, colleagues and relatives, and performing healthful activities like picking up litter, collecting for charity or planting trees.

Oliver Twist
by Charles Dickens

The second novel by Charles Dickens (1812–1870), written when he was just twenty-five years old.

Dickens demonises underprivileged working-class youths who are groomed into becoming criminals in this story of an orphan who joins a pickpocketing gang. Aged nine, Twist is sent to a workhouse, where he is mistreated and deprived of adequate nutrition, in a kind of 'misery memoir' that wallows in a kind of inverted food porn.

Under the tutelage of the Artful Dodger, he gets a place on an informal internship programme in burglary, a key growth industry of the era. After many trials and tribulations, Twist is in the end 'saved' by being welcomed into the bosom of a middle-class household, upholding a view of systematic classism that offers no solutions to the inherent problems of social immobility, simply reinforcing it through a narrative of the upper-class saviour and the lower-class miscreant.

Potential trigger warnings:

! Food poverty
! Absence of a living wage
! Depiction of inner-city smoke pollution alienating to many climate-conscious Londoners, after the successful implementation of ULEZ
! Equally in danger of outraging outer-city car owners unfairly penalised by ULEZ overreach
! Irresponsible characterisation of child gangs as cheerful, welcoming and supportive groups
! Overwritten sentences
! Abandonment issues
! Victim blaming
! Claustrophobia/Fear of chimneys
! Depictions of Jewish people with Irish names

Problematic quotations

'The law is a ass' (sic): promotes poor grammar; 'an' is the correct indefinite article to use before a word beginning with a vowel. Further, to modern readers 'ass' is a colloquial term for a bottom. Suggest changing to: 'The law is a donkey'.

'Please, sir, I want some more': stigmatises those living in food poverty. Danger of encouraging enlarged portion sizes, which goes against acknowledged obesity guidelines. Suggest changing to: 'Please, sir, is this one of my five a day?'

Suggested revisions

The character of Nancy should be aged up to eighteen, as reference to the existence of child prostitutes is not suitable for a work of entertainment.

Fagin is an antisemitic stereotype. His character should be changed to a plump, cheerful man from Lancashire.

Most sentences are too long to be understood by modern readers. Suggest cutting all of them in half or rewriting using ChatGPT.

Younger readers will be traumatised by descriptions of the life of London's poor – make these characters more comfortable, healthy and in less physical and psychological danger, to protect readers' mental health.

The Tale of Peter Rabbit
by Beatrix Potter

No other text covered in this book deserves as much urgent and complete overhauling as this supposedly 'cutesy' tale, in which Peter disobeys his mother to go exploring in Mr McGregor's garden to try to find food, and is nearly caught. Probably it has so far escaped attention owing to the gentle tone of its artwork and the supposed safeness and simplicity of the story – this is exactly how the very worst offenders against our values have evaded censure for so long, by hiding 'in plain sight'.

The Tale of Peter Rabbit (aimed, according to the publishers, at ages three to six) actually belongs in the horror genre, and is specifically an 'ordeal horror' narrative. It is bizarrely identical in narrative structure (and indeed several plot details and twists) to rural horrors such as *The Texas Chainsaw Massacre* and *The Hills Have Eyes*.

After wandering into Mr McGregor's yard, Peter is hunted, trapped inside a shed among garden machinery, repeatedly escapes death by the narrowest of margins, and at times can only *hear* the sound of the approaching murderous weapon (in this case Mr McGregor's hoe): 'scr-r-ritch, scratch, scratch, scritch' it goes as it comes ever closer to his hiding place – a classic horror trope.

At last he is reduced to tears of pure terror. And although he finally escapes with his life, Peter's clothes, which he has left behind, are placed on a scarecrow as a ghastly effigy, a frequent sight in scary films across the decades.

That Beatrix Potter was a deeply disturbed individual is not in question. Perhaps she truly believed herself to be telling innocent tales about the foibles of fluffy woodland creatures, and was unaware of the harm she was wreaking. Whether one can plausibly speculate that she was in denial or constructed this disturbing narrative out of sheer perverse malevolence is hard to say, and for each of us to decide in our own hearts.

Potential trigger warnings

! Onion intolerance
! Fur allergy
! Fear of scarecrows

Problematic quotations

'Fuck a duck – that McGregor shitbag's a real cunt!' – apparently a deliberate piece of sabotage by a discontented employee at the printer's works, this only appeared in the first edition, and was exorcised in later print runs.

Understandably, original unexpurgated copies now change hands for high sums, but obviously ought not to be read to children.

Suggested revisions

There is a clear theme of childhood deprivation in the tale. In fact, it is about Peter's determination to escape from poverty: Peter's mother goes off to buy food for the other children, purchasing unhealthy bread and buns (indigestible for rabbits). However Peter, on his own initiative, finds and eats radishes, French beans, lettuce and parsley – he clearly has a natural culinary instinct and taste which could be his ticket out of privation. At the tale's end he ought to get a scholarship to catering college.

Peter's membership of the non-privileged underclass is clear from his slipshod ways and the fact that he wears a flashy new coat (bright blue with brass buttons), which is clearly a status symbol, with the buttons as 'bling'. Emphasise this, with him wearing very low-slung jeans showing his underwear, gold jewellery and having him spitting conspicuously in front of strangers.

Mrs Rabbit's unsuitability as a mother is made clear, not only from the poor diet she gives her children but from the fact that she leaves them completely unsupervised while she goes to the bakery, a trip which seems to take some time. She also (astonishing in a book once considered suitable for infants) tells Peter that his father was murdered, butchered, cooked in a pie and eaten: a savage and deliberate piece of mental cruelty which probably leaves life-long scars and carries with it a dark threat of cannibalism. Suggest that social services pay a visit at the end of the book to discuss her catalogue of failings.

The Bible

The Old Testament

As the bestselling book of all time (the Old Testament is usually published in one volume along with its even more successful sequel), the harm spread by this absolute ... well, *bible* of patriarchy is incalculable. With its male God overseeing all, and then passing on control to the original nepo baby, Jesus Christ, who simply promotes a more left-wing version of his father's ideology (who knows how far and how quickly his views might have migrated rightwards had he lived beyond the age of thirty-three?), it provides a pattern of abusive power structures that has stayed in force to this day. It is crammed back to front with bad messaging on almost every level.

To enumerate all the ways in which the Bible ought to be updated would take a volume longer than the original. However, here are the most salient points that ought to be considered from the most famous parts.

Noah's Ark

It is harmful to depict animals (and to presume on their behalf that they would so choose) in marital units of two, as though all animals mate for life, which is not the case. However, seeing as the book is for a human readership, the animals ought to be depicted in a wide-ranging style of coupling, with different numbers and types of partners in each. Indeed, the number of animals in the Ark enables every acceptable type of adult relationship in the modern world to be depicted so as to be inclusive to all and not be judgemental to any.

The Commandments

These should be called the 'polite suggestions', as 'commandment' sounds coercive.

1. 'I am the Lord your God, who brought you out of the Land of Egypt and out of bondage, you shall have no other gods before Me' – reference to bondage is inappropriate. Change to: 'I released you from the gimp mask of the Pharaohs.'
2. 'Thou shalt not make any graven images' – engraving is an honourable and helpful profession, and it is hard to understand what the original objection may have been. Delete this.
3. 'Thou shalt not take the Lord's name in vain' – the meaning of 'taking in vain' is obscure language to modern readers. Normally something happening 'in vain' means that it fails, but here it means

'inappropriately' or 'disrespectfully', which leads to misunderstandings. Change to: 'Thou shalt not exclaim "Jesus Fucking Christ!" when thou hits thy thumb hammering in a nail.'

4. 'Remember the Sabbath Day and keep it holy' – it is wise advice for people to make the most use they can of their precious Saturday; nevertheless, readers who don't fully subscribe to the whole 'God actually exists' narrative of the Bible could be alienated by this. Change to: 'The Sabbath Day is precious, easily frittered away on mindless nonsense – don't waste that, mofo! #bestlife.'

5. 'Thou shalt honour thy father and thy mother' – few sentiments have dated so much so suddenly as this, in a generation where we are fully starting to understand the incalculable harm done by poor parenting. Replace with: 'Give your mother and father the benefit of the doubt; they are only people, and by the law of chance probably didn't completely ruin your life just for shits and giggles, but because of their own shortcomings.'

6. 'Thou shalt not kill' – it is now widely agreed that euthanasia is a humane practice and so this 'commandment' is out of date. Replace with: 'Killing should definitely be frowned upon but can be carried out in the correct consensual circumstances and in a professional environment in line with strictly enforced regulatory guidelines.'

7. 'Thou shalt not commit adultery' – many marriages can be loveless and stifling, or even still loving but sexless, and many mental health professionals would

hesitate before endorsing a blanket ban on adultery, which can be an emotional refuge for persons in genuine distress. 'Don't fuck around' would be better.

8. 'Thou shalt not steal' – this is fine.
9. 'Thou shalt honour the Lord thy God' – repetitious, delete this.
10. 'Thou shalt not covet thy neighbour's ox' – beef livestock are well known to contribute large amounts of harmful greenhouse gases, and a widely available book such as the Bible should definitely not be promoting it as something to be coveted. Nevertheless, a healthy amount of envy can be a useful motivating force for self-improvement, within reason. A sensible compromise would be: 'Thou might be allowed to covet somewhat thy neighbour's solar panelling, but don't let that shit get out of hand.'

Lot's Wife

The moral tale of Lot's wife being saved from the city of Sodom, only to be turned into a pillar of salt when she looks back at the city's holy destruction is alarming in dietary terms. Excessive salt causes high blood pressure and risk of stroke. The text should be changed to something more health-conscious, such as low-sodium salt, or a block of powdered turmeric (the benefits of which are well documented).

The New Testament

Conveyed in its purest and most simplistic form – reduced to the rubric of the Golden Rule – the message of Jesus Christ (or Yeshua) appears not to have aged a day. Who can argue with: do not treat others as you would not wish yourself to be treated? Look closer, however, and there are multiple clumsy, wrong-footed pieces of messaging and many downright dangerous elements in the New Testament . . .

The Nativity

Joseph accepting the cosmic fatherhood of Mary's baby at her word is implausible and inappropriate: he ought to request a paternity test, which (if the Bible is indeed the word of God) the baby's real father would be eminently capable of providing, presumably on a block of stone.

On reaching the inn in Bethlehem and finding it full, Joseph should threaten to leave a negative review on Tripadvisor and leverage some additional extras to make the stable more comfortable, such as room service.

The appearance of the Three Wise Men is openly misogynistic and ableist. One should be a woman, one non-binary, and all should be of differing levels of intelligence.

The benefits of home-birthing are well documented, but there should be a trained midwife present. The stable is not strictly a 'home', except to the collection of donkeys, goats and cattle. However, if the inn was – as it may well have been – the ancient Judean equivalent of an Airbnb, it is entirely plausible that it would be referred to as a 'granny annexe' – change text to reflect this.

The Good Samaritan

It is clear to the present-day reader that this parable in large part excuses widespread racism or xenophobia, as it accuses *nearly all* Samaritans of being incapable of good deeds, which (despite the hopeful message of the tale) may expose distasteful prejudices in both the teller and the audience of the original tale. Suggest this is changed to 'The Good Random Bloke on the Street'.

The Wedding Feast at Cana

We do not know whether alcoholism was a widespread problem in first-century Judea. Aside from Noah's problematic inebriation in the Old Testament, alcohol addiction is not frequently addressed in the Bible. Nevertheless, the presence of huge flagons of wine, and the fact that it all gets drunk – at the wedding feast at Cana – strongly hints at the issue. Either way, alcohol abuse must not be encouraged when there are some simple fixes to hand. Jesus could just as easily turn the urns of water into alcohol-free wine. Or, if it is alcoholic, he could encourage drinkers to alternate their wine with glasses of water. He could counsel people about their alcohol use and inform them of the long-term health risks of sustained alcohol consumption. (Admittedly, the effectiveness of this late at night at a wedding feast might be doubted.) Best of all, and even more magical than creating wine, he could turn the water into some healthful drink the guests have never drunk before and would enjoy – such as kombucha.

The Feeding of the Five Thousand

No tale from the life of Jesus has dated as suddenly as this story of forcing five thousand hungry individuals to eat a meal of fish and bread. Current statistics indicate this would be thoroughly inappropriate for as much as 40 per cent of the diners, whether through food intolerances or dietary choices. A wide variety of options ought to be provided and therefore Jesus should ensure well in advance that food stalls are in place to offer gluten-free, vegetarian and vegan options, with of course rigorous and clear signage for anyone with allergies to sesame, wheat, nuts, ancient grains (referred to at the time simply as 'grains'), fructose, lactose, salicylates, amines and short-chain carbohydrates.

Walking on Water

While Jesus joins the disciples on their boat and helps them land an enormous catch of fish, it should be made clear that this is in line with replenishable fishing quotas in the Red Sea at the time, and that none of the types of fish caught were endangered. His walking on water could also be seen as irresponsible and risking the lives of others by setting a dangerous example. He ought to say: 'Don't try this at home! To be clear, only I can do this because I'm God's son!'

The Sermon on the Mount: The Beatitudes

As usual, Jesus's words come from the right place but need to be updated to make sense to a contemporary audience and to avoid any misunderstanding, which could have disastrous consequences.

'Blessed are the poor in spirit' – this is vague and unhelpful. A more up-to-date and precise mandate would be, 'Blessed are those who suffer from anxiety, depression, sleep deprivation, stress, low self-esteem, racing or uncontrollable thoughts, heart palpitations, workplace bullying, financial or food insecurity, generalised fear, chronic doubt and severe emotional fatigue.'

'Blessed are those who hunger and thirst after righteousness' – this is dangerously subjective, as many controversial and problematic figures consider themselves to be righteous individuals. Suggest cutting and replacing with, 'Blessed are those who go out of their way to offer their services free of charge or out of hours, such as legal aid or emergency dentists.'

'Blessed are the merciful' – looked at from any angle, it's difficult to find a problem with this one.

'Blessed are the pure in heart' – this is highly subjective and could give encouragement to people with dangerous agendas. Change to: 'Blessed are those who do their best to try to maintain a sense of objectivity.'

'Blessed are the peacemakers' – a Peacemaker is a type of gun. Also, notoriously, many former winners of the Nobel Peace Prize turn out to be extremely problematic, so change 'peacemakers' to 'conflict-alternative-solution specialists'.

The Death of Jesus

The Last Supper

The Apostles should split the bill evenly between them, leave at least a 12.5 per cent tip, and also enquire as to whether tips genuinely get paid to staff.

The Garden of Gethsemane

Judas kissing Jesus in the garden after dark is a golden (or rainbow 😊) opportunity to update the text and make it friendly to modern audiences by including a moment of LGBTQI+-friendly sex-positive content. The garden is clearly a place where men feel able to kiss each other under the cover of darkness, and the subtext is clear: there were safe spaces for gay men at the time in Jerusalem.

The arrest of Jesus by the authorities immediately afterwards could then be given another layer of meaning, which is a brutal police crackdown on an oppressed minority, given extra resonance by Jesus's words, 'Love one another, *as I have loved you.*'

The Mount of Olives which stands near Gethsemane could in this entirely logical interpretation of the text be imagined to be a lesbian bar. And although this author is exceeding their strict brief in adding this, of course, in a stage adaptation one would be tempted to include singers coming out in rainbow loincloths and singing 'INRI' to the tune of 'YMCA', as a protest song against the retreating Roman soldiers!

Pontius Pilate

When brought in front of Pontius Pilate, Jesus gives only cryptic answers to the questions. It would be more in keeping with 2024 policing that he should be read his statutory rights off a scroll before being subjected to psychological torture, lies and manipulative interrogation methods. In a modern translation which people would understand, Jesus should just say, 'No comment.'

The Dictionary

One of the favourite moves of the gleeful troublemakers who champion the 'anti-woke agenda' is to enjoy 'saying the unsayable', to trumpet certain phrases and words that are harmful for the sheer joy of doing so, just because they ought to be allowed.

No book sums up and encourages this antiquated, poisonous outlook better than the Dictionary, which proudly expounds and explains every politically incorrect term and every hate-filled concept under the sun. It lays these weaponised words out for all to see, callously arranging them beside each other alphabetically, as though all words are equal and due the same respect and value.

Naturally, if one wants to look up a racist epithet or derogatory term (although why you would want to is not at all apparent), one might do so by exploring the more dank and foetid corners of the internet, and/or by working out meanings via context.

But it cannot be right in a just and equal society (or one that makes hopeful gestures towards being so) that such terms are available to all, even the smallest child, fully explained and given historical roots, as though that is the most natural thing in the world. The very presence of the book on book-shop shelves is a tacit acknowledgement that such concepts and terms are acceptable, and not to be shunned.

It is only a matter of time before right-thinking people understand this cannot continue, that evil things can only be removed by *their being removed*. Before too long the fact that any such thing as a dictionary ever existed will be seen as yet another shameful shadow on our past that we are relieved we have finally left behind us, just like the thousands of instances of evil it proudly endorses.

Movie Titles:
Inclusivity Watch

Today, many movies of yesteryear now thankfully come preceded by trigger warnings to acquaint the contemporary audience that the films were made when societal values were very different. However, it has so far been overlooked that movie titles themselves often clearly display hurtful, damaging and regressive attitudes.

In light of this, it would be best practice to initiate a process relating to historical movies and begin combing libraries for titles that can be helped to be made safe – for their own future security. Here are a few humble suggestions offered up by the author as a first step.

Title	Suggested alternative
Dial M for Murder	*Dial M for Mediation*
Faster, Pussycat! Kill! Kill!	*Take a Valium and Meditate, There's No Need for Violence*
Tinker, Tailor, Soldier, Spy	*Yoga Instructor, Retail Assistant, Barista, Spy*
The Picture of Dorian Gray	*The Doctored Selfie of Dorian Gray*
Hideous Kinky	*Unconventionally Attractive Sex Positive*
Killers of the Flower Moon	*End-of-Life Assistants of the Flower Moon*
The Men Who Stare at Goats	*The Men Who Stare at OnlyFans*
Mindhunters	*Mindfulness Hunters*
Chappie	*Chappie GPT*

Title	Suggested alternative
Fried Green Tomatoes at the Whistle Stop Cafe	*Avocado on Toast at the Whistle Stop Cafe*
Marathon Man	*Couch-to-10k Dad*
The Postman Always Rings Twice	*The Postman Only Rings Once Because You Only Get One Phone Call from Prison*
Sex, Lies, and Videotape	*Netflix and Chill*
How Green Was My Valley	*How Green is My Windfarm?*
Bring Me the Head of Alfredo Garcia	*Please Have Alfredo Garcia Report to HR for Retraining*
Dude, Where's My Car?	*Dude, Let's Take the Bus!*
The Loneliness of the Long-Distance Runner	*The Improved Mental Health of the Person Who Takes Regular Strenuous Exercise*
Bang the Drum Slowly	*Remain Within Sound Pollution Legislation Guidelines*

Title	Suggested alternative
Dirty Dancing [Trigger: germophobia]	*Clean Dancing*
Close Encounters of the Third Kind	*Social Distancing of the Third Kind*
Mutiny on the Bounty [Trigger: sugar consumption]	*Mutiny on the Sugar-Free Oat Bar*
The Godfather	*The Cis-male Non-denominational-deity Parent Surrogate*
White Men Can't Jump	*Assumptions on People's Ability to Jump Should Not Be Made Based on their Gender or Ethnicity*
Lawrence of Arabia	*Inappropriate Self-Appointed 'White Saviour' of MENA*
Mad Max	*Highly Motivated and Resourceful Max with Anger Issues*

Title	Suggested alternative
Lara Croft: Tomb Raider	*Lara Croft: Artefact Returner and Apology Deliverer*
My Big Fat Greek Wedding	*My Sensible Healthy Mediterranean Civil Partnership Ceremony*
The Best Exotic Marigold Hotel	*The Best Entirely Normal to Native Dwellers Unbranded Washing-up Gloves Hotel*
Eat Pray Love [Note: the title of this movie and book, written in the imperative voice, as though to tell the reader/viewer what to do, is already out of date]	*Intermittently Fast, Practise Mindfulness, Be Self-Partnered*
Never Let Me Go	*Respect My Personal Space*
Friends with Benefits	*Friends Whose Rights to Receive Employment Relief is None of My Concern*

Title	Suggested alternative
Beauty and the Beast	*Two Persons Whose Names Do Not Adequately Represent Their Inner Worth*
Crazy Rich Asians	[Holy shit, nothing can be done with this]
Call Me By Your Name	*Call Me By the Name I've Respectfully Asked to Be Addressed By*
Psycho	*Person with Treatable Psychiatric Condition*
Scarface	*Tony Montana*
Snow White and the Seven Dwarfs [Title gives a false impression that Snow White is separate and above her friends]	*Bashful, Doc, Dopey, Grumpy, Happy, Sleepy, Sneezy and Snow White*
Planes, Trains and Automobiles	*Bikes, Trams, Car-sharing and Not Travelling Unnecessarily*

Film History:
The Sensitivity Read I

Many of the most famous scenes from film history, when watched back, still have a great deal of power – to upset, that is, owing to how poorly they've dated. Here are some sensible initial attempts to sanitise the worst offenders and de-fang the most triggering moments so that we can still enjoy these masterpieces safely.

Scene change #1: *Reservoir Dogs*

The opening diner scene in *Reservoir Dogs* is decidedly un-pleasant to watch – six white males listen while Quentin Tarantino (Mr Brown) gives a lengthy speech about the possible meaning of Madonna's song 'Like a Virgin'. It is extremely distasteful for a current audience (indeed it is a wonder how any of the men are able to hold down their breakfasts while listening to such concentrated misogyny) and a preferable version is offered here:

[INT. A DINER. DAY.]

The camera prowls around the men as they eat breakfast at a circular table.

>   MR BROWN
> So, what I'm saying is, she's,
> like, a virgin, right? That's what
> she's saying.

>   MR ORANGE
> Go on . . .

>   MR BROWN
> And that's where my interest
> ends. That's her business. What's
> a man like me doing getting
> interested in her private life?

>   NICE GUY EDDIE
>   *(Eating a forkful of waffle)*
> Quite right.

>   MR BROWN
> She's a successful recording
> artist, a self-made woman. I
> should respect that. The lyrics –
> who knows what they mean.

                    MR PINK
        (Contemplating his plate of eggs)
        Who are we to plumb the depths of
        an artist's heart?

                    MR BROWN
        Who indeed? Now that is dealt
        with, would anyone like some more
        bacon?

                    MR BLUE
        I'm watching my cholesterol.

                    MR BROWN
        Very wise.

Scene change #2: *Goodfellas*

The character of Tommy DeVito (Joe Pesci), as depicted
in Martin Scorsese's *Goodfellas*, is a key player in the New
York mafia. He is an enforcer and a killer, with a hair-trigger
temper. In one famous scene set in the middle of a busy
restaurant, Tommy makes his friends (primarily Henry Hill –
played by Ray Liotta) laugh uproariously and then pretends
to lose his temper at their laughing at him, threatening them
with his gun – a terrifyingly accurate portrayal of mascu-
line controlling behaviour. It is also notably disrespectful to
clowns. It should be changed in future versions of the film.
Here is a more tasteful and sensitive alternative:

[INT. RESTAURANT. NIGHT.]

TOMMY has been regaling the assembled wise guys with a choice anecdote. They are all weak with laughter and wiping tears from their eyes, especially HENRY HILL.

          HENRY
Tommy, you're a funny guy, I tell you what.

          TOMMY
Me? Funny? Funny how?

          HENRY
You're just funny, is all.

          TOMMY
Yeah - but funny how? You mean I make you laugh, like I'm some kind of clown?

          HENRY
No, I didn't mean that.

          TOMMY
Well, that's a shame because clowning is a noble profession which goes back centuries, and is a more sophisticated and complex

41

art than people commonly give it
credit for.

          HENRY
Tommy, I hear you. Nevertheless,
I was not comparing you to a
clown.

          TOMMY
But funny how? Like I'm a
performer? I make you laugh?

          HENRY
Laughter relieves tension and
enhances social relationships.
Therefore, I commend you for
increasing the overall human
happiness by bringing the gift of
laughter. Also, it doesn't mean I
respect you less because you are
amusing.

          TOMMY
Nor would I assume that you
did mean that! However, it's
kind of you to think to offer
me a compliment. I am sincerely
grateful and I respect you as a
colleague.

                    HENRY
        As I do you.

                    TOMMY
        Hurray!

Scene change #3: *Taxi Driver*

Martin Scorsese's 1976 film is a parable of inner-city societal
alienation and spiritual decay. The infamous scene where
Travis Bickle (Robert De Niro), the titular taxi driver, stands
in front of a mirror having a sequence of conversations with
imaginary assailants is a powerful expression of male despair
that has lost none of its eloquence in the fifty years since it
was made. This is why it should be changed, to offer a more
hopeful and empowering message to the youth of today.

[INT. BEDROOM. DAY.]

                    TRAVIS
            (To the mirror)
        You talking to me?

Pauses.

                    TRAVIS
        You talking to me?

He turns round in mock surprise to look
behind him.

                        43

                    TRAVIS
        I'm the only one here. Are you
        talking to *me*?

Pauses.

                    TRAVIS
        Oh, you are. Good! Maintaining
        clear lines of communication is
        important for positive mental
        health outcomes. Hop in the cab
        and tell me where you want to go,
        my friend!

He gives an enthusiastic thumbs-up and a
wide reassuring smile, then puts his leather
coat on to go back to his cab in a more
cheerful spirit.

Scene change #4: *Braveheart*

William Wallace led an uprising against the tyrannical rule
of the English King Edward I in 1297. His rebellion was
brutally crushed. Mel Gibson's 1996 film *Braveheart* won
five Oscars, including for best film and best director, but it is
grossly historically inaccurate in almost all of its details, including costume, make-up and the events portrayed. A more
accurate version would be far more respectful to the history
of the Scottish nation:

[EXT. A FIELD. DAY.]

WILLIAM WALLACE rides his horse in front of his troops and rallies them before the final attack against the English forces at the Battle of Falkirk.

> WILLIAM
> Fight with me this day, and you may lose your lives! But if you *don't* fight . . .

Turns horse and rides back along front line of soldiers.

> WILLIAM
> You will remember on your deathbed you gave up this one chance . . . to tell the English that they may take our lives, but they'll never take . . . OUR FREEDOM!

Crowd cheers as he raises his sword above his head.

> WILLIAM
> That said, as an abstract concept, 'freedom' is relative. Because we are going to be thoroughly defeated, and

eventually tricked into becoming
one country with the English in
1707, until eventually at the
end of the twentieth century,
we will receive devolved powers
from Westminster. For what that's
worth.

Crowd goes quiet, listening.

> WILLIAM
> (Clears throat) And although
> there will be a plebiscite for
> an independent Scotland, a
> 'yes' vote is a very dubious
> prize because we will be
> financially beholden to England's
> contributions to our welfare
> system owing to widespread
> unemployment and healthcare
> issues including high rates
> of depression and substance
> dependency, which is another
> kettle of fish entirely . . . So,
> be careful what you wish for, I
> suppose . . . But now let's go and
> fight those English!

Crowd half-heartedly gives assent.

Scene change #5: *The Shining*

Near the culmination of Stanley Kubrick's adaptation of Stephen King's masterpiece, the maddened author Jack Torrance (Jack Nicholson) takes an axe and chops down the door of the bathroom in which his wife is hiding, in fear for her life – a deeply upsetting scene which must be altered.

[INT. HOTEL. NIGHT.]

WENDY TORRANCE cowers in the bathroom, whimpering and clutching a carving knife.

Outside, her husband JACK TORRANCE wields an axe. He swings it heavily over his head and it smashes into the door. The tip gets lodged between two planks. WENDY screams.

> JACK
> Little pigs! Little pigs! Let me in! Not by the hair on my chinny-chin-chin!

He levers the blade out of the door and swings it again with even more violence. The whole head of the axe thunders through a panel of the door.

> JACK
> Then I'll huff, and I'll puff, and I'll blow your house in!

WENDY screams at the top of her voice.

          JACK
*(Peering through the hole in the
door he has just made)*
Oh, hello darling. I didn't
realise you were in there. I was
just going to get rid of this
door and replace it, as you asked
me to. No time like the present
for pushing on with a spot
of DIY!

          WENDY
It was a tad alarming, Jack!

          JACK
I do apologise. I was just also
rehearsing bedtime stories for
when I put Danny to bed later.
'The Three Little Pigs' is one of
his favourites. By the way, I've
made you a hot-water bottle.

          WENDY
That's very considerate of you.
Possibly consider knocking and
asking politely before smashing a
door in with an axe next time?

JACK

Of course I will. I can't imagine
how I was so thoughtless. Thank
you for the advice.

WENDY

My pleasure, dear.

Beowulf

The first poem composed in English (written c. CE 600–900, but set centuries earlier). Author's identity unknown.

Beowulf, a 'mighty warrior', is a mercenary who is hired to murder Grendel (a person suffering from gigantism and/or possible acromegaly), a misunderstood societal outsider. The epitome of toxic masculinity, Beowulf then proceeds to murder Grendel's mother, reinforcing outdated ideas of patriarchal power structures and inherent misogyny.

Instead of being punished for these egregious actions, Beowulf lives for fifty years as the chief of his 'clan', a group that lives completely isolated from the outside world (giving uncomfortable overtones of maintaining 'racial purity'). When Beowulf self-centredly goes for one last 'adventure' to slay a dangerous dragon, he is killed, leaving his entire people facing oblivion, simply because (the text insultingly implies) they lack a powerful man to protect them.

Potential trigger warnings

! Overbearing/overprotective maternal relationships between Grendel and Grendel's mother could be triggering for people with similar experiences
! The text overtly approves of swords and bladed violence, which is very problematic in today's high-crime culture
! Dragon's jealous accumulation of treasure is a clear attack on those suffering from hoarding disorder
! The murder of a dragon will distress readers with pet lizards; equally, dragons are a rare and precious species which ought to be protected and celebrated, rather than ignorantly culled
! The poem was written in English, but is set in Denmark and Sweden and is therefore guilty of cultural appropriation

Problematic quotations

'They have seen my strength for themselves,/Have watched me rise from the darkness of war,/dripping with my enemies' blood': deeply inappropriate for a character to be drenched in blood – will cause nightmares and long-lasting mental health implications in many readers. It should later be revealed that Beowulf has been selflessly taking part in a blood-donation drive, and the stain is just a single droplet covered with a bandage.

'Then Beowulf spoke – on him the armour shone, the

mail-shirt linked by the skills of the smith': The very epitome of that harmful cliché, the 'knight in shining armour', an explicit encouragement for headstrong cis-males to assert themselves over others' narratives. A much less overbearing costume would mitigate Beowulf's self-importance, which is stifling to other voices (in both the story and the readership). Suggest changing to skinny jeans, a loose-fitting unbranded tee, sneakers and a hoody.

Suggested revisions

The Mead Hall being the focal point of human society encourages alcohol consumption. Suggest altering to an Oat Milk Hall.

The characters are almost all men, who only ever talk about war. This is gendered and retrograde; suggest including *women* talking about war, and men talking about their feelings and being supportive of one another.

Grendel's mother lives at the bottom of a swamp, and Beowulf has to swim downwards for two days to reach her lair. This is both unrealistic and may encourage children to risk their lives holding their breath underwater for too long.

'Beowulf' as a protagonist's name evokes macho stereotypes: beer and wolf. Contemporary audiences will be unable to relate to this nominative braggadocio; better to call the character something that sounds more gentle. Sticking to the formula of a drink paired with an animal, perhaps 'Flat-White Badger' would do.

Grendel's mother's swamp location encourages prejudice against endangered wetland ecosystems and the health benefits of wild swimming. Her abode in the text should be moved to somewhere considered villainous to modern eyes, for example a castle with zero thermal insulation, terrible energy efficiency and no council recycling service.

SpongeBob SquarePants
(United Plankton Pictures)

Brightly coloured SpongeBob has already been enmeshed in his own little culture war when a few American politicians threw red meat to their red-state voters by suggesting banning him on the grounds of promoting homosexuality, a laughable charge. In fact, SpongeBob should be banned (or very drastically rewritten) for entirely different reasons.

The example set by the show is reprehensible, focusing as it does on such a clearly emotionally unstable young creature, and forcing him into multiple situations he cannot deal with. He is unable to cope with the most minute setbacks and weeps torrents of tears, runs around screaming, and experiences uncontrollable jubilation, often within a few moments of each other. He is literally an emotional sponge, and a sensitive treatment of him would be to have him given therapy, possibly medication such as Ritalin, and perhaps placed in a permanent educational facility to give him stability and improve his future prospects.

The idea of his working in a burger restaurant is worrying

not just for the saturated fat and unhealthy over-salted foods that surround him, but also because the Pacific Ocean setting means that a Hawaiian-themed poké restaurant would be far more culturally appropriate.

A final note is the concerning obsession with underwear in the show, which is inappropriate and must be removed: he lives in a place called Bikini Bottom and the name 'SquarePants' makes him patronymically defined by his undergarments, which is undoubtedly wrong. SpongeBob's surname should reflect his heritage and be chosen from the most common surnames in Hawaii: Wong, Smith or Yamamoto.

Julius Caesar
by William Shakespeare

Shakespeare's 1599 play about the death of one of the greatest military tacticians of all time and the internecine violence that followed is a tragedy in more ways than one. Aside from a story of regicide (or czar-icide, if you will) it is a dire warning of what happens when you leave a whole civilisation in the hands of bloodthirsty selfish careerist alpha bros – a worthy message, for sure. However, it contains a plethora of wrongheaded elements that can be improved by a few easy fixes.

Note: owing to an oversight in title choice, many readers or audience members fail to realise that Shakespeare's *Antony and Cleopatra* (1606) is a sequel to *Julius Caesar*. Suggest in future that the later play is retitled *Julius Caesar 2*.

Potential trigger warnings

! Knife crime

! Fear of togas
! Mob violence

Problematic quotations

'Friends, Romans, countrymen – lend me your ears': unfair
to those with hearing disorders, and more so to those
with missing outer ears. Also sexist and presumptuous.
To be understood by present-day audiences, it should be:
'Acquaintances, strangers, people of all genders – please like
and subscribe.'

'Et tu, Brute?': could be misunderstood as asking Brutus
if he's had lunch. Would help if it was far more direct and in
the contemporary vernacular understood by working-class
audiences, instead of in Latin: 'You stitched me up, you filthy
slag!', for instance.

'Cry havoc and let slip the dogs of war!': to use dogs to
embody the ferocity of war is to reinforce unhelpful stereotypes when they are, in fact, loyal companions and givers
of reassurance and physical warmth, especially in a lonely
Norfolk cottage on a cold winter's night when a depressive
academic is trying to complete a book about trigger warnings
on a tight deadline for an editor who is little short of satanic.
'Let slip the commissioning editors of war' would have a more
convincingly sinister sound.

'This was the most unkindest cut of all': this is clearly
ungrammatical and does not promote good and healthy use
of English. It is also unclear (all cuts presumably being at the
very least severely unkind); should be changed to: 'This was
like a real wtf moment.'

'You yourself are much condemn'd to have an itching palm': sufferers of eczema and psoriasis can hardly find this anything other than cruel and insulting. Delete.

'Tear him for his bad verses': this image of a writer being torn to pieces by a crowd for his poor poetry sends a chilling message to the arts. Instead, change his job to one that a mob might more justifiably react to murderously – traffic warden, perhaps, or Chief Executive of Southern Water.

Suggested revisions

The concept of the Ides of March is incomprehensible to twenty-first-century readers; it ought to be changed for another recognisable event usually to be found in the month of March. 'Beware the going forward of the clocks', for instance, 'Beware the FA Cup Quarter Finals' or 'Beware the Easter Monday Bank Holiday because the traffic's always a mare'. Any of these would be suitable.

It's implausible that modern readers could understand a Senate where nothing gets done, resulting in governmental shutdown, legislative logjam and with members openly encouraging insurrection. Instead, the setting should be changed to something more relatable (and likely to be a commercial hit with audiences) like bureaucratic infighting at a paper manufacturer in Slough, or a dysfunctional hotel in Torquay where Caesar is the hapless hotelier.

The play fosters an atmosphere of paranoia within the workplace that could be harmful. Instead, Caesar's death should be an accident, caused by him falling backwards on to Brutus's sword during a trust-building exercise.

The Weather Forecast
(multiple channels)

Possibly the most important of all television programmes in the world, and set to become ever more so over the coming decades, the presentation of the Weather Forecast is deeply outdated and incorrect in its approach and delivery.

The constant barrage of cosy euphemisms and soothing simplifications for the weather patterns delivered by calm, healthy and smartly dressed presenters amounts to deliberate lying to viewers that the situation is somehow okay, and that they are not sleepwalking towards their own obliteration and inevitable slaughter.

It ought to be replaced by specific and clear analysis of what is actually happening to the earth, presented in an appropriate emotional register, i.e. by a person with clinical depression, or by one screaming with terror and with her or his clothes on fire, or drowning in a tank.

Paddington
(Film 2014, dir. Paul King;
from the books by Michael Bond)

Created by Michael Bond in his 1958 book *A Bear Called Paddington*, Paddington Bear has become beloved the world over. Yet like so many creations of the 1950s, there are elements which are distasteful or disturbing for many present-day consumers, even despite the rapturous reception for the *Paddington* movies.

Potential trigger warnings

Marmalade sandwiches: these are packed with sugar, butter/saturated fats and carbohydrates, and ought not to be advertised to children as the favourite food of a beloved main character. Celery sticks would be far more appropriate.

Problematic quotations

'Darkest Peru': this is very troubling language; it is 'othering' to native Peruvians. A character from such a place must only be written by a Peruvian author. Instead, it makes sense for the bear to be from a station that feeds into London Paddington and thus be given *that* place's name. The series of books and films might therefore be renamed *Totnes Bear*, *Bristol Temple Meads Bear* or *Didcot Parkway Bear*.

Suggested revisions

Paddington Bear is a stowaway on a boat – he is an illegal immigrant. In the contemporary climate, a note attached to him reading 'Please look after this bear, thank you' is very unlikely to form a persuasive basis for an application for permission to remain. If the above suggestions about him being made an English bear are not taken up, then the first book ought to be rewritten showing his struggles to fill in paperwork and enduring the refugee-status application process.

Star Wars Episode IV: A New Hope (1977, dir. George Lucas) & *Star Wars Episode V: The Empire Strikes Back* (1980, dir. Irvin Kershner)

The phenomenon that is George Lucas's *Star Wars* universe spans a vast array of movies, TV series, video games, comics and, of course, merchandise: its cultural impact has no equivalent. George Lucas's frequently displayed willingness to go back and change his old works is encouraging, as there are many worrying aspects that warrant reappraisal.

Potential trigger warnings

Claustrophobia: the Trash Compactor scene could be very distressing for sufferers from claustrophobia. The scene should instead be set in an open, airy place like a cafeteria, where the characters are being brusquely ushered out by insensitive staff.

Bad workspace environment: the *Death Star*, and indeed nearly all Empire facilities which are shown, have monotonously bleak and blank décors which psychological studies have shown would likely be depressive and adversarial to positive mental health outcomes for a large proportion of the many thousands of workers who have to inhabit them day by day. Instead, it ought to have posters on the walls with colourful, informative and positive messages, as well as information sheets encouraging soldiers to look after their mental health and consult their physicians in case of difficulties with moods.

Workplace bullying and appropriate remedial action: Darth Vader's treatment of his employees is physically harmful and also has a negative impact on cohort morale. It is likely to suggest bad HR practices in viewers with positions of middle-management who lack the requisite training. Instead of using the Force to restrict the air passage of an officer who is struggling in his role, Vader ought to mentor him and get him to talk through his decision-making process along with being verbally encouraging and offering positive reinforcement.

Problematic language

The 'Force' is an aggressive and coercive term for something intended to represent spiritual peacefulness and balance; suggest change to the 'Pleasant' or the 'Lovely'.

Yoda's speech is clearly mocking those with low education levels, poor achievement in grammar and syntax, as well as a multitude of motor and speech impairments. Suggest that he speak very clearly, and possibly even impatiently correct other people's grammar – behaviour which is recognisable in a wise elder and teacher.

Character name: it is revealed that Obi-Wan Kenobi has been staying incognito under the name 'Ben'. The clear ethnic disparity between these two names in earth languages (one Anglophone, the other sounding Japanese) brings up an uncomfortable suggestion of cultural appropriation and that Obi-Wan (who is from another generation, after all, and having lived in a desert for decades is not au fait with the latest cultural norms) has changed his ethnic identity, which will make many viewers uncomfortable.

Suggested revisions

Jabba the Hutt is a hurtful depiction of a money-lender as a slave-owning criminal with bad personal hygiene. In fact, money-lending is a time-honoured profession which employs millions of people around the world, the large majority of whom are law-abiding individuals who do not deserve to be slandered in the forum of public opinion.

The uniforms of Empire Stormtroopers in the original trilogy are plain white, which implies a complete racial unity among them. This is alarming and upsetting. CGI should be used to grade the colours of the soldiers' armour, showing equal opportunities across the galaxy for soldiers of all shades to join up, as well as inclusive bright rainbow hues, especially during Pride, although it's not clear when this is celebrated in the unnamed galaxy.

There is a dangerous insinuation that having one's arm cut off below the elbow is a minor inconvenience causing little pain and no apparent blood loss, which could encourage impressionable viewers into risky behaviours.

Treasure Island
by Robert Louis Stevenson

The violent, rum-soaked, seafaring *Treasure Island* is the tale of a young Jim Hawkins taking a below-minimum-wage position on the schooner *Hispaniola*, searching for the treasure of the legendary Captain Flint, and falling under the wing of the violent one-legged and one-eyed cook Long John Silver.

The book created a new stereotype of the dastardly pirate: hyper-masculine (also all cis-male), aggressive, self-centred, brutish and unwashed. This became the universal cliché of the golden age of piracy but has now been exposed as a harmful fiction.

In fact, it's well documented that many pirates, indeed several of the most feared and successful, were women. There were people of colour, too, on pirate ships, and the economy practised among pirates was a form of proto-communism where all spoils were shared with absolute equality. With this in mind, it behoves us to reflect with sadness on the anti-pirate agenda espoused by Stevenson, and to speculate why he insisted on pursuing it contra the available evidence.

Potential trigger warnings

! Vertigo – Stevenson invented walking the plank
! Ableism – Long John Silver has severe mobility issues and visual impairment. It is problematic and ableist that only the villain of the story has these challenges. However, it is patronising to those with similar challenges to imply that they *could not also* be villains. Obviously we must avoid giving anyone a false 'halo effect'. Therefore, suggest all characters in the book – good or bad – have one eye and one wooden limb.

Problematic quotations

'Fifteen men on a dead man's chest': it is implausible that fifteen full-grown adult men could stand on the torso of a human male, and deeply inappropriate for them to make an attempt. Or, indeed, that they could fit on the lid of even the most capacious wooden chest or casket. It is difficult to suggest a suitable alternative to this line, but 'fifteen men playing a game of touch rugby' or 'fifteen men spending quality time with their loved ones and being good listeners to their colleagues' would send a healthy message.

'Yo ho ho and a bottle of rum': a plausible verse in a sea-faring shanty but not appropriate in a book aimed at children. Current regulations would recommend changing to, 'Yo ho ho and a cup of reduced-sugar squash.'

'If it comes to swinging, swing all, say I!': nothing could make clearer the stark discrepancies manifest between the values of 1880s Edinburgh and today; reference to swinging must obviously be taken out of a current children's book. However, 'non-standard' family arrangements must not be seen to be demonised. At a stretch, the quote might read: 'If it comes to it . . . perhaps we could explore the possibility of a thruple.'

Suggested revisions

'The black spot' is given to Billy Bones as an indication that his association with his colleagues has been formally severed. This should be changed to a P45 or referred to as a 'final written warning from HR' (which indeed it is).

The character Ben Gunn is revealed to be suffering from severe mental health implications after being 'marooned' on a remote island. This will be severely distressing for those still suffering from the after-effects of isolation during Covid. To prevent this, the island should have a beachside health facility, possibly also with a swim-up bar, so that Gunn's predicament does not cause suffering in the reader.

Winnie-the-Pooh
by A. A. Milne

First introduced in a poem in 1924's *When We Were Very Young*, Winnie-the-Pooh became one of the world's most beloved children's fictional creations for his kindly demeanour, fondness for honey and gentle philosophising. But there are dangers lurking in the Hundred Acre Wood ...

First, it is unquestionably inappropriate for the main character in a children's story – even one that has, until now, been so universally embraced – to wear a jumper on his top half and nothing on the bottom. Aside from whatever it might say about the unsavoury proclivities of A. A. Milne, which have so far gone uninvestigated, it sets a bad example for young readers.

It is a mark of elitism for the stories to be set in a place called the Hundred Acre Wood, considering many readers will not have the opportunity to visit a wood. Strongly recommend that the name be changed to the Hundred Acre Housing Estate.

The modern reader cannot help but see a subversive agenda

at play in the Pooh stories. Central characters are clearly intended to mock people with varying forms of neuro-divergence and mental health challenges: Eeyore embodies depression, Rabbit chronic anxiety, Tigger has ADHD or is perpetually in the 'up' phase of bipolar disorder, Kanga and Roo represent 'split personality' or dissociative identity disorder. The damage done to generations of children by these rude caricatures is incalculable, and that Milne has escaped censure for this for so long is breathtaking.

Potential trigger warnings

! Youth violence – wielding sticks and throwing them from bridges, as well as Christopher Robin shooting Pooh twice while trying to burst the balloon he is hanging from
! Bee stings and anaphylaxis
! Vertigo and falling from trees
! Fear of balloons
! Eating disorders
! Lack of impulse control
! Type 2 diabetes – caused by eating large amounts of honey
! Claustrophobia – being trapped in a rabbit hole
! Body-shaming – being unable to get through a door

Problematic quotations

'If bees are for anything, they're for making honey': in fact, bees operate in a societal structure with complex communication tools and a sophisticated hierarchy – this is disrespectful to them. Change to: 'Bees are very impressive and I'd like to learn more about them.'

Suggested revisions

As noted above, the personalities in the Hundred Acre Wood represent a wide spectrum of psychiatric, mood and personality disorders. Instead of going on reckless adventures, getting stuck in windows and falling out of trees, it would be much more beneficial if they engaged in group therapy.

It is sadly obvious that Pooh is in denial about his serious addiction to honey. He ought to get addiction counselling and gradually be weaned off, possibly onto a less harmful substitute such as sugar-free sweeteners.

The scene where Pooh steals honey from the bees is troubling. Bees are endangered and eliminating their food source threatens destabilising the food chain. In line with the cost of living crisis, Pooh ought to be trying to get honey from a food bank.

It is not accurate that the animals could in reality be friends. A more realistic portrayal would help children's understanding of the natural world. In it, Pooh – a brown bear – would rampage through the wood, killing and eating all of the other characters, including Christopher Robin, before being euthanised by armed police.

Jaws

(1975, dir. Steven Spielberg)

Steven Spielberg's adaptation of the Peter Benchley best-seller is about the hunt for a rogue male great white shark that has been attacking the holidaymakers at Amity Island, on the New York coast. It perpetuates a pernicious myth that nature is an enemy to be feared and that sharks are a major danger to human life, which they are not: tin openers are responsible for more deaths per annum than sharks. Women and people of colour feature in the film hardly at all except as foodstuffs for the shark, although the pusillanimity of local American governance is convincingly portrayed. Other than that, the film needs a thorough re-examination.

Potential trigger warnings

! Outsize meal portions (sharks suffer from
  obesity too)

! Lack of adequate sunscreen protection
! Tuba solos

Problematic quotations

'You're going to need a bigger boat': encourages greediness and acquisitiveness, approving of the waste of nature's resources in building ever vaster super-yachts to service the egos of the ultra-rich.

Suggested revisions

The opening sequence depicts a young girl going swimming in the sea. She ought to wear armbands and a life preserver or adequate breathing equipment in order to swim safely off the coast, whether or not in shark-infested waters.

The famous musical tuba motif makes the shark seem menacing and horrific. This is an inappropriate anthropomorphism as at that moment the shark is simply going about its natural life processes and is no more aware of being 'evil' than a human is when eating a slice of bread. Demonisation leads to humans having a harmful interaction with their own biome. Change to a light, cheerful jazzy score which probably better reflects the shark's actual interior emotional landscape.

Sound of fingernails scratching on blackboard is impossible for many to endure. Suggest changing to an alternative form of ASMR, possibly Richard Dreyfuss whispering into a microphone or sloppily eating a bowl of custard.

The first shark to be caught by the residents of Amity turns out to be have been innocent of the killings – a ghastly piece of animal cruelty. Recommend a scene be inserted in which it is given a respectful burial attended by all the fishermen and -women of the town.

Forrest Gump
(1994, dir. Robert Zemeckis)

Showered with Oscars on its release, *Forrest Gump* is a film that could not be made today, taking as it does the premise of laughing throughout at a person with significant learning challenges and autism-spectrum disorder. It also displays with a shameless lack of criticism the ease with which a white straight cis-male can rise to the top of society on multiple occasions and in widely differing circumstances without either ability or the relevant qualifications.

Potential trigger warnings

! Hurtful to individuals unable to run
! Hurtful to individuals able to run but not long distances
! Insulting to those able to run long distances but not the entire coast-to-coast USA route

! Encourages eating of shrimp, an extremely
allergenic foodstuff deadly to thousands

Problematic quotations

'Run, Forrest, run!': ignoring the spurious fact that this
scene turns out happily for Forrest (which gives the dangerous lesson that children should rely on an implausible turn
of good luck), this is an egregious instruction to give to a
child wearing metallic leg braces. Suggest change to: 'Walk
extremely carefully, Forrest, while I fetch a responsible adult
to scare away those bullies!'

'Life is like a box of chocolates, you never know what you're
gonna get': this statement is famously and woefully inaccurate
as all boxes of chocolates contain printed cards explaining
the different types, or have menus on the inside of the lid.
Chocolates are also very unhealthy and consumption can lead
to type 2 diabetes, tooth decay and heart disease. Equally, the
West's destructive addiction to palm oil is ripping up millions
of miles of rainforest essential to the survival of life on earth,
destroying the habitats of native tribes and leaving millions in
the supply chain trapped in modern slavery – hardly a matter
for whimsical philosophising. Change to: 'Life is filled with
risk, ethical dilemma and compromise, and a vast majority
of people don't have the chances I have had.'

Suggested revisions

The film contains a depiction of a spinal birth defect being cured by running and sheer determination. This is deeply misleading and could give rise to misunderstanding among sufferers of various conditions, not to mention a dangerous distrust of conventional medicine.

Movie Titles:
Inclusivity Watch 2

Title	Suggested alternative
The Postman Always Rings Twice	*The Hermes Delivery Driver Doesn't Even Ring Once*
Pretty Woman	*Woman*
Cat on a Hot Tin Roof	*Cat Safely Indoors in an Air-Conditioned Apartment*
They Shoot Horses, Don't They?	*If It Is Necessary to Put Horses Down It Should Be Done by a Humane Method*
Last Tango in Paris [Obesity guidelines]	*Last Sparkling Water in Paris*

Title	Suggested alternative
The Hangover [Alcohol consumption guidelines]	*The Good Night's Sleep*
Twelve Angry Men	*Twelve Even-Tempered Individuals*
The Fast and the Furious	*The Slow and the Sensible*
Fiddler on the Roof	*Someone Who Takes Tax Accounting Seriously Sitting Behind a Desk*
Goodbye Mr Chips	*Hello Mr Salad*
Sex and the City	*Sex and the Fifteen-Minute City*
Dumb and Dumber	*Two People*
No Country for Old Men	*People of All Ages Are Welcome*
Kiss Kiss Bang Bang	*Smile Nod Gentle Tap Consensual Embrace*

Title	Suggested alternative
It Could Happen to You [Lottery use and gambling guidelines]	*You'd Be Better Advised Saving Your Expendable Income for Emergencies and Healthcare*
Free Willy	*Let's Try to Rescue the Whale*
Nuns on the Run	*Religious Devotees Taking Exercise*
White Hunter Black Heart [Distasteful white/black dichotomy]	*Rich Film Director Shoots an Elephant*
Robin Hood: Prince of Thieves	*Robin Hood: Meritocratically Appointed Leader of Opportunistic Independent Contractors*
Natural Born Killers	*Killers whose Crimes Are Probably Partly Due to a Wide Range of Societal Problems*
The Usual Suspects [Potential profiling]	*A List of Suspects Evaluated with Strict Fairness and Not Judgementally Based on Their Past Deeds*

Title	Suggested alternative
Annie Get Your Gun	*Annie Apply for an ID Check and Wait for the 48-Hour Cooling-off Period to Elapse*
Everyone Says I Love You	*Everyone Upvotes, Likes and Subscribes*
Fear and Loathing in Las Vegas	*Balanced Thought Processes and Mental Health Awareness in Las Vegas*
The Great Train Robbery	*The Irresponsible and Violent Train Robbery*
Midnight in the Garden of Good and Evil	*Midnight in the Non-Judgemental Safe Space*
The Grapes of Wrath	*The Courgettes of Diplomacy*
The Good, the Bad and the Ugly	*Three Individuals About Whom Subjective Judgements May or May Not Be Made on Several Levels*
Whatever Happened to Baby Jane?	*Baby Jane's Legal Right to Be Forgotten*

Title	Suggested alternative
The Dirty Dozen	*Twelve Soldiers Who Should Be Granted Access to Sanitary Facilities*
Seven Brides for Seven Brothers	*Seven Life Partners for Seven Siblings*
My Own Private Idaho	*Idaho, Which I Acknowledge I Have No Personal Claim Over*
Valley of the Dolls	*Uncanny Valley of the Dolls*
Who Framed Roger Rabbit?	*Who Shamed Roger Rabbit?*
Women on the Verge of a Nervous Breakdown	*Women Who Are Recovering Well Despite Suffering Significant Psychological Distress*

Film History:
The Sensitivity Read II

Many of the most famous scenes from film history, when watched back, still have a great deal of power – to upset, that is, owing to how poorly they've dated. Here are some sensible initial attempts to sanitise the worst offenders and de-fang the most triggering moments so that we can still enjoy these masterpieces safely.

Scene change #6: *Spartacus*

After the slave revolt he has led against Rome has ended in defeat, former gladiator Spartacus (Kirk Douglas) is rounded up with the final few thousand slaves by the resurgent Roman troops. But the finest moment of Stanley Kubrick's film comes when the Romans attempt to force the thousand slaves to point out their leader. The scene would be far more appropriate today with one slight change . . .

[EXT. FIELD. DAY.]

The defeated slaves are seated in chains across a valley, surrounded by Roman soldiers on horseback. A SENTINEL approaches.

> SENTINEL
> I come bringing good news from your leader, Marcus Licinius Crassus. You slaves will be spared crucifixion if you give up the person who is known as Spartacus!

The crowd stirs. SPARTACUS looks thoughtful, considering.

> SENTINEL
> Tell us which one he is! And you shall be spared!

SPARTACUS gets up, but before he can open his mouth his dear friend ANTONINUS rises and speaks.

> ANTONINUS
> I identify as Spartacus!

SPARTACUS looks at him aghast.

84

                    SLAVE #1 *(three rows
                    behind)*
I identify as Spartacus!

                    SLAVE #2 *(on the other
                    side of the valley)*
I identify as Spartacus!

                    FOUR SLAVES *(in unison)*
I identify as Spartacus!

Disparate slaves across the valley join in
with the chorus. Then all of them rise,
saying the same words.

                    SENTINEL
Very well then! I fully
acknowledge your right to do so!
And as a show of respect, also,
and perhaps I ought to have
said this earlier, you shall no
longer be slaves! Slavery is a
loathsome institution which must
be abolished!

                    SLAVES
Yay!

85

Scene change #7: *Blade Runner*

The death scene of Roy Batty in Ridley Scott's 1982 science-fiction masterpiece is one of the most frequently quoted scenes in cinema, where a sentient machine suddenly realises in the final moments of his mortality what it has meant to be alive. However, it would be sensitive to younger audiences (facing a world emptied of opportunity by the older generation) if the scene was rewritten to acknowledge that the character played by Rutger Hauer (1944–2019) had a sweeter life than they have any chance of looking forward to.

[EXT. ROOF. NIGHT.]

Neon lights refract through the rainwater..
The replicant BATTY has been wounded and is
dying. He has moments to come to terms with
his fate.

> BATTY
> I've seen things . . . which you
> couldn't imagine. Attack ships
> on fire off the shoulder of
> Orion. Space beams glittering at
> the Tannhäuser Gate. Affordable
> house prices and a buoyant jobs
> market. More astounding than any
> of these – a final salary pension
> scheme . . . lifelong financial
> stability . . . a peaceful Europe

and a holiday home in the South
of France.

He looks around him in disbelief that it's
all ending.

>   BATTY
>   And now those memories will be
>   lost like tears in rain. But it's
>   been a pretty good run, to be
>   quite honest. Being a boomer's
>   pips! What a life! Time to die!
>   Toodle-oo!

Dies at peace with his destiny.

Scene change #8: *On the Waterfront*

Terry Malloy (Marlon Brando) is coming face to face with the
fact he's been forced to give up his hopes and dreams of being
a great boxer, just to be a strong-arm union man in the New
York boatyards for his brother Charley (Rod Steiger). He'd
been fighting the realisation until now – and when it comes
it's one of the most heartbreaking realisations of working-
class male hopelessness ever put on screen – so powerful it is
likely to reinforce negative self-image in the youth of today
and ought to be rewritten and re-shot with the help of CGI,
with a more hopeful message.

[INT. TAXI CAB. NIGHT.]

          TERRY
It ain't right, Charley. I coulda
had class! I could have been
somebody! I could have been a
contender!

          CHARLEY
Don't say that, Terry. You're
young, after all. Take adult
education. You can get an NVQ or
GNVQ! Go to night school, get a
training qualification and start
a new career. Statistics show
these are consistently effective
methods of improving your long-
term prospects, although it will
certainly take hard work.

          TERRY
You think I could have a chance
in another career?

          CHARLEY
Take your pick!

          TERRY
This is certainly encouraging.
Thank you for your helpful words.

                    CHARLEY
Naturally I want you to continue
knocking heads for me in the
(frankly corrupt) union business
down by the docks. But I know
better opportunities for you lie
elsewhere.

                    TERRY
I was glad you said it rather
than me. Your honesty does you
great credit!

                    CHARLEY
Good of you to say.

Scene change #9: *American Pie*

Desperate to know what penetrative sex feels like, and having been told that it feels like warm apple pie, the virgin Jim has just come home to an empty house to find a recently de-ovened apple pie on the counter top. Jim's father enters the house a few minutes later to interrupt Jim and the pie in a decidedly compromising position. However, on discovering his son's attraction to pastry goods, Jim's dad does not provide him with the supportive messaging that would these days be appropriate and expected.

[INT. KITCHEN. DAY.]

JIM'S DAD comes in and sees him. He looks surprised.

>   JIM'S DAD
> Jim, what are you doing there?

>   JIM
> Dad! Oh my God! I thought you were out!

>   JIM'S DAD
> I came back early.

>   JIM
> Oh Jesus!

>   JIM's DAD
> Well, Jim, this is nothing to be embarrassed about. Clearly you are at the very least pie-curious. Humans are sexually attracted to all different kinds of things on this earth, and it behoves us to acknowledge this sensitively without making individuals feel like outcasts.

>   JIM
> I see.

90

JIM'S DAD

There are probably a large
number of people out there who
feel exactly as you do. Long-
lasting and fulfilling sexual
relationships with pastry
products are no doubt *de rigueur*
in some quarters, and I have no
intention of 'yucking your yum'.
You must follow your feelings and
not allow others to cause you
to doubt your inclinations or
experience inward shame. After
all, the field of human sexual
experience and desire is as broad
and varied as the contents of any
bakery window.

JIM

That's great!

JIM'S DAD

Great indeed. We shall begin
at once. Whether a pie can give
informed consent is of course a
moot point but that is no reason
for me or anyone to stand between
you and erotic and emotional
bliss. I wish you happiness.

91

                    JIM
You're the best!

                    JIM'S DAD
Okay, now here's a cloth, wipe
yourself down - this is a
kitchen, after all.

Scene change #10: *Field of Dreams*

Although *Field of Dreams* is an inspiring tale in which Kevin
Costner's character Ray Kinsella decides to build a baseball
field because a ghost whispers in his ear, it cannot be denied
that Mr Kinsella undertakes a risky venture with a strong
chance of failure and places a significant burden on his family
without their consent. The dangers should be made clear to
the audience so that others are not encouraged to take the
same steps recklessly.

[EXT. FIELD. DAY.]

RAY KINSELLA walks away from his house into
the corn, which stretches over his head. All
of a sudden he hears a gentle whisper.

                    WHISPER
If you build it, he will come ...

RAY turns round, confused and disorientated.
He calls to his wife.

                    RAY
          What was that voice?

His WIFE and their SON are on the swing
chair on the veranda. They both shrug, they
haven't heard anything.

                    WHISPER
          If you build it, he will come . . .

                    RAY
          You mean, if I build a baseball
          diamond, it may turn out to
          attract a world-class ball player
          to these parts, bringing fame and
          fortune to this quiet spot and
          make a grand story to be told for
          generations afterwards?

                    WHISPER
          In a word, yes. However, I should
          warn you that 90 per cent of
          new business start-ups fail and
          leave the owners saddled with
          terrible debt.

                    RAY
          A baseball pitch, you say?

                    WHISPER

Well, yes, but bear in mind you
have no planning permission and
will have to take out large loans
on the security of your home. The
workload alone will be enormous
and the stress it will put on
your marriage considerable.
Think extremely carefully before
you make a next step - take
independent financial advice and
never make a serious financial
commitment without considering
very carefully and making sure
you have a back-up plan. Also you
really should get a brain scan to
make sure your hearing things is
not a worrying sign of a medical
problem . . .

                    RAY
I love baseball! Let's do it!

                    WHISPER
        (Sighs)

Scene change #11: *The Fugitive*

Although the Harrison Ford vehicle is a thrilling game of cat
and mouse, in fact the main character (wrongfully convicted

murderer Dr Richard Kimble) relentlessly breaks the law in his pursuit of justice, and despite appearing to be cleared of his original crime at the end of the film would in reality still be facing a multitude of additional felony charges including theft, resisting arrest, assault, breaking-and-entering and appropriation of medical records, which would add up to a considerably longer sentence than a conviction for murder. It would be far more acceptable to show audiences that in defiance of movie heroics the best route to freedom is, after all, to apply oneself to the various available routes through the legal system.

[EXT. STORM DRAIN. DAY.]

Fugitive Dr RICHARD KIMBLE has stumbled through the sewers pursued by the FBI. Coming round a corner he comes face to face with a seven-hundred-foot drop where the drain empties out down the side of a dam. There is no way forward, or back.

Behind him appears FBI Agent SAMUEL GERARD, hard at his heels.

> GERARD
> Put that gun down! Put that gun down now!

KIMBLE slowly and reluctantly does so, his hands shaking. Trying to look for a way out.

                    GERARD
        Hands up! Do you want to get
        shot? On your knees!

                    KIMBLE
        I didn't kill my wife!

                    GERARD
        I don't care!

Water rushes past their feet and cascades
out into the air, as GERARD creeps forward,
gun raised.

                    GERARD
        However, if you have been falsely
        incarcerated there are options
        available to you. Over and above
        the multiple-level appeals process
        which goes all the way to the
        Supreme Court, there are numerous
        charities such as the Innocence
        Project, which take a close look
        at historical murder convictions
        to which serious doubts still
        attach.

                    KIMBLE
        Is that so?

                    GERARD

Indeed! Best to trust in the
processes of the law rather
than run away and risk dying of
hypothermia or being killed by
the gun of a policeperson.

                    KIMBLE

You make a compelling argument.

                    GERARD

I'm gratified that my message is
getting through. Although the
wheels of justice move slowly,
there is hope at the end of the
tunnel. The metaphorical tunnel,
I mean, not this physical one!

                    KIMBLE

Ha, ha.

                    GERARD

Also, eff why eye, although a
fictional film could show you
jumping from such a height as
this and surviving, trust me, in
real life you *would* definitely be
killed.

                    KIMBLE
Hmm. Pop on the cuffs then, if
you would.

                    GERARD
Certainly will, matey.

1984
by George Orwell

Like many an instinctive and passionate hard-left socialist, George Orwell's heart was in the right place (albeit his lungs were in dire straits) when he was writing *1984*. Its depiction of a frightening totalitarian futuristic regime was a resonant warning to several generations of readers, mentally arming them against the evils of communist states such as the USSR. However, the year 1984 is long behind us, and many of the things Orwell warned about have come to pass and proved to be but minor intrusions, some entirely harmless and even fun!

After all, who has not enjoyed watching the television shows *Big Brother* and *Room 101*? Victory Gin (the acrid state-produced liquor which makes Winston Smith burp) is now a drink marketed with apparent lack of irony to a joyful guzzling public. More important, Orwell's vision of a populace under constant surveillance by powerful outside forces is a reality that is here to stay, and which it is fruitless to rail against.

Potential trigger warnings

! Fear of rats
! Cigarette addiction
! Hibernophobia – the only Irish character in the book (O'Brien) is its villain. Suggest adding at least one other Irish character to even this out, possibly a kindly female neighbour who always pats Winston Smith cheerfully on the back and says, 'Cheer up, it might never happen!' with a jolly chuckle.
! Unprotected sex
! Kink-shaming – Winston and Julia are observed having sex in a bluebell wood and humiliated for it. Instead, this healthy and sex-positive behaviour should be tacitly endorsed and their privacy respected.

Problematic quotations

'It was a bright cold day in April and the clocks were striking thirteen': the idea of a 'cold' day in April is fast becoming out of date. Change to 'alarmingly stifling'.

Suggested revisions

Tone: the book would make much more sense to a contemporary audience as a romantic comedy with plenty of social media interaction. There is a romance; a happy ending could easily be added. Winston Smith gives in, in the end, to long-term commitment!

Room 101: the rats in the cage scene – so effective in the original – could be replaced by a CAPTCHA system where he has to click certain items in the correct order on a screen to prove he is not a computer program and get through to the message from Julia confirming their love for each other.

As it stands, the book's depiction of blanket surveillance encourages paranoia, which could be harmful to readers' mental health. Add a few instances where Winston finds it 'strangely comforting' that he knows he is a good person and has nothing to hide, or (or as well as) a few instances where he feels a twinge of unease but knows he can't do anything about it and so shrugs it off. A more plausible addition would be a friend who freaks out and tries to go 'off grid' whom Winston could regard with weary contempt.

In the world of Airstrip One, novels are made by novel-writing machines – yet another astonishing prediction by Orwell which is on the brink of coming true, if it isn't true already at time of publication. This should be taken further, with AI being credited for all writings, and newsreels which Winston Smith watches should show all authors and journalists being rounded up and sent for 'retraining'.

Dear Zoo
by Rod Campbell

There are many supposedly innocent texts in this book which are disturbing on closer inspection, but perhaps none comes close to the sheer weirdness of Rod Campbell's lift-the-flap book for pre-school infants. Even the most superficial analysis of the story, and the values it espouses, would leave one speechless.

The story is of a first-person narrator who for some reason 'orders' a pet from the zoo (apparently refusing to specify which animal is wanted) and receives a sequence of unsafe animals through the post: elephant, giraffe, lion, camel, snake, monkey and frog. The narrator sends each of these back, finally receiving a puppy.

The rules of this fictional world are filled with despair and abuse. Who is running this so-called 'zoo', which sends out rare, precious, vulnerable and dangerous animals to domestic households? Why do they continuously send out random animals one after the other instead of finding out what the customer wants? With such managerial incompetency, one shudders to imagine what other neglect and malpractice may be in operation at the zoo. Better to ask: what actually are 'zoos' in this fictional universe?

But the questions do not stop there. Why does the postal service allow such things to be shipped at all, and why – as is clearly shown in the book – in boxes only just large enough to contain the poor creatures, who must undoubtedly arrive in a state of physical and emotional trauma? It is unquestionably a form of animal cruelty.

The narrator's placid acceptance of events and relaxed indifference to the animals' fate is as appalling as any other factor. And finally one arrives at the blanket misogyny of this world where all animals are male, meaning any infant being read to will equate maleness with being a representative of one's class, and femaleness with being invisible or inconsequential.

Suggested revisions

If *Dear Zoo* must be suffered to exist at all (and not banished to some underground museum of depravities) the narrator should view and learn about the animals in their natural habitats, and their genders should reflect modern society.

Matilda
by Roald Dahl

One of the most popular books by one of the world's most revered children's authors, *Matilda* features a precocious four-year-old heroine blessed with temporary supernatural powers with which she terrorises a respected pillar of the community (her headmistress, no less), causing what appears to be a complete mental breakdown.

It is around the character of the headmistress, Miss Trunchbull, that the book's problematic attitudes reveal themselves. Miss Trunchbull is a single woman of extraordinary personal achievement (proudly representing her country at athletics), succeeding in a male-dominated field, but is particularly mocked for her stature, which doesn't comply with traditional notions of feminine beauty, and for her manner, which is admirably forthright and direct.

The book is openly hostile to the idea of a woman showing strength – both physical and mental. The plot revolves around historical allegations against her for which there is no shred of proof in a court of law or out of it, and the manner in which audiences have responded with glee to the mental abuse suffered by the impressive Miss Trunchbull is sadly typical of the kind of uncontrolled mob-mentality extra-judicial 'social justice' campaigns which have been shown to cause such havoc and distress.

Potential trigger warnings

Gaslighting: Miss Trunchbull is submitted to a deliberate, detailed and elaborate plan to make her believe that she is being watched by a ghost, a situation which Matilda's accomplice, Miss Honey, once aware of, does nothing to prevent.

Problematic quotations

'Never do anything by halves if you want to get away with it': typical of the deception practised by nearly all the characters in the book, and amounts to a kind of spiritual slogan underlying the entire project.

Suggested revisions

The scenes detailing Matilda's father, Mr Wormwood's business activities are practically a detailed course in criminal practices and must be struck out. Instead, he ought to be an honest broker working hard to get his customers the best deal. Other inappropriate scenes abound: showing young readers where to find newts and how to use them to cause emotional distress to hardworking professional teachers; placing itching powder in drawers full of knickers; putting syrup on adults' chairs; plus a pervasive untruthfulness in dealings with adults. All these passages ought to be altered to portray appropriate behaviours.

The passionate and committed Miss Trunchbull admittedly has certain shortcomings when it comes to anger management, no doubt due to the social pressures she has had to overcome to reach her station in life. She ought to be sympathised with for this rather than demonised, and to receive therapy and counselling.

A Christmas Carol
by Charles Dickens

The perennial Christmas favourite appears to be a perfect festive tale, showing as it does the emotional rebirth of a cold-hearted and selfish individual. However, this is in truth a tale of terror, a Gothic home-invasion story, in which an elderly and physically vulnerable protagonist is repeatedly terrorised – deliberately given to believe he is suffering from poisoning, hallucinations and persecution.

The fact that Scrooge emerges with an apparently positive mental outcome is a fact of random chance and certainly not the result of any carefully monitored treatment path or in accordance with therapeutic best practice. After all, are these Christmas spirits intending to perform regular check-ups on Scrooge, to ensure that his recovery maintains its course and he won't (like so many extreme cases, after a brief window of recovery) return to his former attitudes, and perhaps worse than ever?

Potential trigger warnings

! Night terrors
! Ghosts and supernatural disturbances
! Burning of coal as domestic fuel source
! Gaslighting: the fact that the terrors Scrooge endures happen via gaslight gives a bitter double-meaning to the term

Problematic quotations

'Humbug!': Mr Scrooge ought to have an exclamation more in line with current sugar consumption guidelines, such as, 'FFS!'

Suggested revisions

The plot promotes Christian worship above other religions, which is inadvisable. Suggest the story is changed to occur over the evening during some secular celebration such as the Super Bowl.

Scrooge's HR practices badly need updating. He fails to comply with working time directives. There should be a scene where the clerks at his counting house unionise, or (more likely) one in which he forces them to sign zero-hours contracts, which are essential in this day and age to ensure continuity for small businesses in a competitive zone.

Scrooge is ahead of his time in not wanting to burn fossil fuels – cutting back to only one coal on the fire. Although he should be displayed investing his savings in a carbon-capture programme.

Ebenezer Scrooge has of course traditionally been cast as the villain of this supposedly 'heart-warming' festive tale. Yet there is much complexity here. He clearly has undiagnosed emotional and psychiatric conditions, undoubtedly based on deep historical trauma, which cause him as much misery as anyone else. In a tale that truly reflects the goodwill of the yuletide season, he would receive help from a trained medical practitioner with whom he would agree a long-term plan for gradual improvement rather than the brief shock-tactic therapy which the spirits enact upon him.

Goldfinger
(1964, dir. Guy Hamilton)

In many ways ahead of its time, this film requires a complete re-evaluation in light of current values. Seen clearly, it is the story of a brave entrepreneur making a brilliant attempt to leverage market value for himself and his investors. Auric Goldfinger is a forerunner of the tech giants of today, his innovative free-market spirit hampered by absurd governmental over-reach in the person of the psychopathic James Bond. He is essentially attempting to create his own crypto-exchange sixty years before it was thought possible, and ought to be lauded as a financial prophet.

Potential trigger warnings

! Body paint
! Fear of hats
! Gold fetishism

Problematic quotations

'Where is Goldfinger?' 'Playing his golden harp': there is no indication that Goldfinger has any musical leanings or ability in the rest of the text. Could be confusing. Change to: 'He flew out of the plane's window and is dead.'

Suggested revisions

James Bond criticises the Beatles, who are universally accepted to be among the greatest musical geniuses of the twentieth century. Implausible and jarring to modern sensibilities. Change to Cliff Richard.

The name Pussy Galore is famously inappropriate and has been mocked by generations of comedians. If reference must be made to sex in the names of Bond 'girls' (cf. Honey Ryder, Miss Goodnight) – and by the way Honor Blackman was forty when she played the role – her name ought to be Ms Genitalia-Incognita.

Goldfinger is depicted cheating at golf, which is an elitist sport most young people do not understand or have knowledge of. It is impossible for modern audiences to relate to a plump, all-powerful orange-haired billionaire who cheats at golf while playing on a course that he himself owns. Suggest Bond and Goldfinger go head-to-head in a skateboarding contest instead.

Miss Moneypenny is depicted as waiting for James Bond to marry her – she states clearly that the only gold she wants is on the third finger of her left hand. This is an insulting diminution of her personhood and independence of thought:

instead, she should be calmly aloof from 007's charms (dubious as they are) and indeed tell him about the exciting weekend she has planned going bodysurfing and/or on a mindfulness retreat.

Film History:
The Sensitivity Read III

Many of the most famous scenes from film history, when watched back, still have a great deal of power – to upset, that is, owing to how poorly they've dated. Here are some sensible initial attempts to sanitise the worst offenders and de-fang the most triggering moments so that we can still enjoy these masterpieces safely.

Scene change #12: *Titanic*

At the close of James Cameron's gigantically successful tragi-romance, the love-struck main characters Jack and Rose are separated by what the film pretends is a heartrending personal sacrifice, but is in fact an unnecessary piece of self-glorification by Jack, who could be experiencing self-doubt about his long-term commitment to Rose or about their future together as a couple in the New World. Simple mathematics or even common sense dictate that any piece of floating wreckage large enough to carry one person is also large enough to carry two, huddled together. A vision with him showing a bit more faith would offer young males a better role model ...

[EXT. ATLANTIC OCEAN. NIGHT.]

ROSE is lying flat on a piece of wreckage. JACK is in the water.

>   JACK
>   Hold on for just a bit longer,
>   Rose. Keep that priceless
>   gem, btw.

>   ROSE
>   Eh? But there's plenty of room on
>   here for you!

>   JACK
>   Don't think of me. I'm going now.
>   You must save yourself, for both
>   of us!

>   ROSE
>   Don't be such a fucking drama
>   queen and make this all
>   about you!

                    JACK
          Eh? I'm so cold . . . It's time for
          me to go . . .

                    ROSE
          Here.

ROSE reaches in, grabs JACK by the collar
and hauls him up onto the wreckage alongside
her. Then gives him a big cuddle.

                    ROSE
          We are statistically far more
          likely to survive the night if we
          huddle together and share body
          warmth. By sacrificing yourself
          you were literally risking my
          life, not saving it.

                    JACK
          I guess that makes sense.

                    ROSE
          Shut up and cuddle me, you
          gorgeous working-class oik.

                    JACK
          I can't help my upbringing. And
          you shouldn't make me feel self-
          conscious for it.

                         115

ROSE

Didn't mean to, soz. Let's keep
ourselves cheerful by singing the
Cheltenham Ladies' College school
song! Come on!

JACK *(Shuddering)*

Of course. I know it well. Remind
me of the words . . .

Scene change #13: *Dirty Harry*

The notoriously right-wing *Dirty Harry* movies, featuring Clint
Eastwood's shoot-first, answer-questions-in-the-mayor's-
office-later detective Harry Callahan became a byword for
swaggering American movie cop violence. However, the most
famous scene is from the first film directed by Don Siegel
in 1971, where Callahan taunts an African American bank
robber to pick up his discarded firearm and risk being shot
dead (depending on how many rounds Harry has left in his
Magnum). In light of recent controversies (or not really – it
should always have been like this) the scene ought to play out
a different way . . .

[EXT. STREET. DAY.]

DETECTIVE HARRY CALLAHAN has chased the
SUSPECT in an armed robbery through the San
Francisco streets, shooting several times. At
last the SUSPECT trips and falls in a shop

116

doorway, his shotgun just inches from his grasp.

CALLAHAN approaches.

>CALLAHAN
>I know what you're thinking. 'Did he fire six shots? Or only five?'

SUSPECT squints up at him, short of breath.

>CALLAHAN
>Well, seeing as this is a .44 Magnum, the most powerful handgun in the world, and could blow your head clean off, you got to ask yourself one question. How much civic damage has he done in the past few minutes, and with what risk to civilian life?

>SUSPECT
>I was wondering, as a matter of fact.

>CALLAHAN
>There will have to be a thorough investigation into my behaviour to judge whether my actions were proportionate and well judged. And you can bet I will

be cooperating with it fully,
as you would have a right to
expect from any employee of San
Francisco City. Of course, I will
be filing my full report, which
will be available for anyone to
view under freedom of information
legislation.

                SUSPECT
Phew, I am relieved to hear it.

                CALLAHAN
You betcha. By the way, don't
touch that shotgun that your
hand has been slowly reaching out
towards.

                SUSPECT *(Withdrawing hand)*
I was starting to think that
might be ill advised.

Scene change #14: *There Will Be Blood*

Paul Thomas Anderson's 2007 multi-Oscar-winning parable about how the self-resilience of the individualistic American male turns to obsession with power and eventually to murder is one of the great films of its decade. The towering performance by Daniel Day-Lewis as Daniel Plainview is a mesmerising whirlwind of psychopathic energy. However, the scene in which he explains his approach to others – where he boasts of stealing someone else's resources with the jubilant phrase 'I drink your milkshake!' – ought to be changed to be in line with contemporary dietary advice.

[INT. PRIVATE BOWLING ALLEY. NIGHT.]

DANIEL PLAINVIEW is in the grip of passion. He towers over the young ELI SUNDAY.

> PLAINVIEW
> Let's just imagine that you
> have a milkshake. And *I* have
> a milkshake. And I have a
> straw which goes from over
> *heeeeeere* . . .

He stalks halfway across the room to indicate the starting position of his lengthy straw.

> PLAINVIEW
> *Allllll* the way over to you . . .

He walks back towards SUNDAY meaningfully, maintaining eye contact.

> PLAINVIEW
> I put my straw into *your*
> milkshake. And I DRINK your

milkshake! I drink it all up! I
DRINK YOUR MILKSHAKE!

The young man is transfixed.

          PLAINVIEW
Do you want to know *why* I drink
your milkshake?

SUNDAY nods.

          PLAINVIEW
Because milkshake is bad for you!
It's got sugar! It's got milk!
It's got maybe ice cream as well!
Young man like you shouldn't be
drinking no damn milkshake! So
I drink it up! And I replace it
with a nice carrot, spinach and
ginger smoothie. That's got good
stuff in it and will make you
grow up all good and strong!

          SUNDAY
Gee, Mr Sunday, that's good of
you. You're really looking out
for me.

          PLAINVIEW
That I am, son. Think nothing of
it! Now, get out of here before I

do something crazy like knocking
your head in with a bowling ball!

SUNDAY *(Scarpering)*
Laters!

Scene change #15: *Basic Instinct*

The scandalous sex-thriller *Basic Instinct*, featuring Sharon
Stone as a crime writer who may or may not also be a sex
murderess, shocked audiences and became one of the highest-
grossing American films at the 1992 domestic box office. It
has a number of famous and (at the time) outrageous scenes
but one in particular is in need of updating . . .

[INT. PRECINCT HOUSE. DAY.]

CATHERINE TRAMELL is being interviewed by
police. She is under suspicion of murdering
multiple people, including her own parents.
She is apparently utterly unfazed – and
glamorous, in a white dress and white shawl.
She languorously lights a cigarette and
exhales the smoke.

DETECTIVE
Can you please extinguish your
cigarette, Ms Tramell?

TRAMELL

What are you going to do? Charge
me with smoking?

DETECTIVE

Yes!

TRAMELL

Oh.

DETECTIVE

It's illegal to smoke in
a workplace in the State
of California. You're in
contravention of several statutes
and local ordnances for which
there is a heavy fine. And if the
fine goes unpaid, possible jail
time. You are threatening others'
health with your smoke!

TRAMELL *(Putting the
cigarette out)*

I stand corrected. Putting
other people's health in danger,
you say?

DETECTIVE

Indeed!

122

                    TRAMELL
    I would feel awful if I did that.

                    DETECTIVE
    Well, there we go. Thank you. Now
    on to these murders . . .

Scene change #16: *Se7en*

Se7en, David Fincher's 1995 ultra-stylish Gothic serial-killer thriller is a work of macabre, malevolent artistry. There are multiple scenes which must cause offence to many, but possibly the most triggering will be where Brad Pitt's character has a box delivered to him containing a decidedly grisly body part cut from someone close to him. It would probably be best if the scene was rewritten to protect audiences from being triggered by the fear of violence against a loved one, perhaps like this:

[EXT. BADLANDS. DAY.]

A mysterious package has just been dropped
by a courier. DETECTIVE SOMERSET bends down
to open it with his knife. When he peers
inside he is shocked. He turns round and
runs back towards DETECTIVE MILLS, yelling
at him to drop his gun.

MILLS is confused. The serial-killer suspect,
JOHN DOE, is handcuffed on his knees. They
both watch SOMERSET approaching.

> MILLS
> What's this . . . ? What's going on?

> JOHN DOE
> I've always wanted to live like
> you, Detective Mills. I envy you.

> MILLS
> Shut up!

> SOMERSET *(from far away)*
> Put your gun down! Mills!

> JOHN DOE
> I paid a visit to your house
> today. I wanted to see how you
> live . . . I met your pretty
> wife . . .

> MILLS
> *What?*

> JOHN DOE
> I felt envious of you.

MILLS *(to Somerset)*
What was in the box? What's in
the box?

SOMERSET
You should put your gun down.
It's . . . a bath bomb. And
some oat cookies. And incense
sticks . . .

JOHN DOE
I knew chasing me must have been
very stressful for you so I made
you some nice little snacks and
bought you some gifts to de-
stress your workplace.

MILLS
You shouldn't have!

JOHN DOE
Oh, it's nothing really. Just a
little gesture. After all, I chose
to do the murders and you didn't
choose to have to investigate
them - it must be a very
difficult time for you. I felt it
was the least I could do!

SOMERSET
You are the sweetest.

125

> MILLS *(Biting into a*
> *cookie)*

These are DELICIOUS! You must
give me the recipe!

Scene change #17: *The Lord of the Rings: The Fellowship of the Ring*

The Fellowship of the Ring have travelled many days through the silent and eerie Mines of Moria. Just as they are within reach of the exit, they have awoken a horde of orcs and killed hundreds of them on their retreat to safety. However, are they being sensitive to local norms? They are trespassing in these caves, after all. As the final conflict begins, it would be best if this was addressed . . .

[INT. HALLS OF MORIA. NIGHT.]

GANDALF THE GREY steps forth onto the bridge
of Khazad-dûm. The Fellowship are all safe
on the other side. But from the shadow they
have left behind steps forth a fearsome
BALROG, a demon of the ancient world – a
creature of shadow and flame.

GANDALF bravely holds his staff aloft.

                    GANDALF
      I am a servant of the secret
      fire! Wielder of the flame
      of Anor!

The BALROG comes closer. It is a hundred
feet tall; furnace flames shoot from its
nose, lava leaks from the cracks in its
skin. It leers down at him and roars.

                    GANDALF
      The dark fire will not avail you,
      flame of Udûn!

The BALROG opens its cavernous mouth and
emits a terrifying roar.

                    GANDALF
      No, but seriously, I'm feeling
      really awkward in case we've
      trespassed or been culturally
      insensitive at all. You know,
      like, when you go on holiday and
      don't know the social rules and
      whatnot. There's nothing worse
      than a bunch of insensitive
      tourists, blundering about and
      offending the locals . . .

                    BALROG
No, you're fine, we're pretty
free and easy round here with
visitors and so forth. No rules
really . . .

                    GANDALF
We killed a bunch of orcs.
Worried that might be a bit of a
faux pas . . .

                    BALROG
Mate, I can't turn around without
stepping on a hundred orcs. They
get everywhere!

HORDE OF ORCS emits a chorus of screeching
howls.

                    BALROG
Oh shut up, you lot. Howl
this, howl that. You don't know
how bloody starved for good
conversation I am down here. Nah,
mate - you see, originally this
was a Dwarven kingdom. We're just
colonialists who've taken it over,
right? So we haven't really got a
leg to stand on.

                    GANDALF
Oh great! Thanks for that. And,
bee tee dubs, when it comes to
not having a leg to stand on, you
know that bridge we were both on
just a moment ago . . .

                    BALROG *(Looks down)*
Oh shiiiiiii . . . *(voice
diminishes as BALROG and GANDALF
fall into pit)*

Scene change #18: *An Officer and a Gentleman*

In the famous dramatic ending of Taylor Hackford's Oscar-winning 1982 romantic drama, Richard Gere's character walks into a busy working factory, comes up behind his girlfriend (Debra Winger), who is literally operating heavy machinery and wearing ear plugs, and startles her with a kiss on the back of the neck. The scene contains a multitude of health and safety breaches that seriously put at risk any viewers who attempted to emulate them. A safety-approved version would be something like this:

[EXT. FACTORY. DAY.]

Newly qualified Aviation Officer ZACK
MAYO walks towards the factory where his
girlfriend PAULA works. He has passed his

officer's exams and is wearing a dazzling white officer's uniform.

He reaches the factory and reports straight to the reception area.

[INT. FACTORY. DAY.]

ZACK signs in and receives a hard hat, a visitor's pass and lanyard, and a bright yellow safety jacket.

A SECURITY OFFICER escorts him to the factory floor.

A SUPERVISOR advises PAULA that there is a visitor and she safely stops the machine where she is working. She steps away from the workspace and goes to a meeting room where ZACK is waiting.

ZACK explains that he has passed his exams and she is very pleased. They hug. After walking outside at a sensible pace, she leaps into his arms and their celebrations may begin.

The Lion, the Witch and the Wardrobe
by C. S. Lewis

C. S. Lewis's Chronicles of Narnia series of children's fantasy fiction has proven enduringly popular, which is to be regretted when one considers the many ways it is unsuitable for young minds of today. In *The Lion, the Witch and the Wardrobe*, the Pevensie children find themselves transported to Narnia, where they are offered drugged Turkish delight and must battle the evil White Witch.

Most famously, the book series is freighted – weighed down almost to sinking – with its Christian message, which ought to be removed. Nevertheless, that is not the text's only problematic aspect, as we shall see . . .

Potential trigger warnings

! Feline fur allergy

! Fear of wardrobes and other enclosed spaces
! Christian messaging

Suggested revisions

Children today do not usually have wardrobes, which are somewhat antiquated objects. Suggest that the magic wardrobe is changed to a magic chest of drawers, or a magic scattering of dirty clothes all over the floor.

It is not appropriate to promote Turkish delight to young audiences, not only because of its high sugar content but also because it can be seen as product placement for Cadbury, and also tacitly approving the unnutritious pink jelly culturally appropriated by Cadbury and sold under the name 'Turkish Delight', which natives of Türkiye would rightly regard with astonished scorn.

Christian messaging: to obviate the New Testament metaphor so obnoxious to any readers who are not practising Christians, and to resonate with a modern secular readership, instead of being sacrificed, Aslan should be sent to a lion sanctuary – it is clear the terrain in this part of Narnia is not suitable for lions even when out of perpetual winter.

Climate change: the permanent winter which the White Witch brings about would be disorientating and bewildering to young readers who these days rarely experience snow. A far better solution would be for the land to be rapidly and dangerously warming up, the signs of which only the less powerful creatures have noticed. Thus the villainous witch could be depicted as an industrialist and lobbyist against climate change solutions (then, the witch could be not white but a witch of colour, improving the book's diversity).

The Pevensie children are sent to the countryside as evacuees from the Blitz: most children do not understand this concept and would be upset if it was explained to them. To be more relatable, make this that they've been driven out of Central London by their privileged father at the beginning of the Covid pandemic, possibly towards Barnard Castle, and dropped with relatives.

Despite being depicted physically as a faun, Mr Tumnus is clearly a distasteful, lazy and offensive stereotype of an Irish person. He has red fur, utters 'To be sure, to be sure!', plays folk music about rivers flowing with wine, is heavily sentimental and bursts into passionate tears at the drop of a hat. To bring this up to date he ought to be a sensible, level-headed businessman proud of his EU passport and with very grave doubts about doing trade with a post-Brexit UK.

The *News*
(multiple channels)

Possibly the longest-running and most popular television programme yet to avoid serious scrutiny has been the so-called *News*. How this is the case is baffling: after all, it comprises a continuous parade of damaging material that is offensive to nearly every conceivable minority or oppressed group.

That it is inexplicably promoted by every major mainstream media channel, considering its harm, is bizarre. Yet it continues to stream through the screens of millions every day, with apparently not a thought for the people it hurts.

Most remarkable of all is the vaunted and deeply dubious 'factual' nature of this programme. Amazing indeed, when every edition exposes the wild inaccuracies of its predecessor. A glance back in time shows that the *News* is not just bad and inaccurate now, but has been from its very start (witness the frequent uncritical coverage of persons who turn out to be deeply problematic). Even quoting any of the endless examples that spring to mind could be triggering for readers.

One can even ask, considering the risk to public mental

health, is there actually such a thing as a news story which it is responsible to broadcast? It is an issue worth exploring.

In all conscience and as things stand, if the *News* is to continue, it can only do so with a comprehensive list of trigger warnings before each episode which cover every potential offence the programme might cause. At a conservative estimate, such a list would take up an equal amount of airtime to the actual stories covered, but would be a valuable exercise.

It might seem extreme or indeed fanciful, but why has the *News* not been put on its final warning or cancelled? It would be simple to replace it with something more progressive, positive and respectful of the mental health of its viewers, such as a collection of stories that theoretically *could* be true, and spread messages of harmony and hopefulness.

Film History:
The Sensitivity Read IV

Many of the most famous scenes from film history, when watched back, still have a great deal of power – to upset, that is, owing to how poorly they've dated. Here are some sensible initial attempts to sanitise the worst offenders and de-fang the most triggering moments so that we can still enjoy these masterpieces safely.

Scene change #19: *Crocodile Dundee*

The scene in which an American street hood attempts to hold up Mick 'Crocodile' Dundee, only to find that the other man has a far larger knife than him, is a famous laugh-out-loud moment in the 1986 fish-out-of-water comedy. This is why it must be removed, as making light of knife crime is in danger of perpetuating that exact same social scourge. A far more acceptable version would be this:

[EXT. NEW YORK STREET. DAY.]

MICK DUNDEE and his friend SUE CHARLTON are walking out from a subway station arm in arm when a THUG jumps out at them.

              THUG
    Gimme your cash!

Mick looks him up and down, unimpressed. The THUG is shivering and on edge.

              SUE
    Give it to him, Mick. He's got a
    knife!

              MICK DUNDEE
    Call that a knife?

              THUG
    Yes, I do.

              MICK DUNDEE
    I do as well, because that's what
    it is. However, knives are very
    dangerous and can ruin lives.
    Just think, what if we got in a
    scuffle and the knife ended up
    being used on you?

THUG

I hadn't thought of that.

MICK DUNDEE

As it happens, I've got a much
larger knife in my belt but
I wasn't going to mention it
because that would be wanton
braggadocio. Let's both throw
away our weapons lest they cause
any more mischief, my man!

THUG

A good idea. I'm glad I met you.

MICK DUNDEE

Now be off with you.

THUG

Maybe I'll go and score some
high-quality cheap cocaine, which
is so readily available on the
streets of New York City, this
being the 1980s after all.

MICK DUNDEE

Don't do that either.

THUG

Okey-dokey!

138

Scene change #20: *Fatal Attraction*

The second-highest grossing US domestic film of 1987, *Fatal Attraction* shows how a one-night stand goes wrong when Glenn Close as a powerful executive (Alex Forrest) invades the family home of Michael Douglas's character, Dan Gallagher. The most famous scene is where it is discovered that the family rabbit has been murdered and left to boil in a pot on the kitchen hob.

Aside from the flagrant animal cruelty, the scene created the misogynistic trope that is the phrase 'bunny boiler' – used to refer dismissively to an unhappily rejected woman. A more appropriate version follows:

[EXT. GARDEN. DAY.]

DAN GALLAGHER walks behind his young daughter through the garden as the girl runs towards the rabbit hutch, and sees it is empty, with its door open.

[INT. KITCHEN. DAY.]

Coming into the kitchen, BETH GALLAGHER sees that there is a pot bubbling over on the stove top. She reaches out and lifts the lid. But then she sees ALEX FORREST standing by the cooker.

                    BETH
          What are you cooking?

                    ALEX
        Rarebit.

BETH screams. Then she sees ALEX is cuddling
the family rabbit in her arms. ALEX puts the
rabbit down, opens the grill, and takes out
a few delicious slices of melted cheese on
toast.

                    BETH
        Sorry to overreact - I thought
        you meant you'd cooked our
        family's beloved pet rabbit.

                    ALEX
        What an amusing misunderstanding!
        The boiling water is for
        peppermint tea.

                    BETH
        Some delicious Welsh rarebit will
        be just the ticket. I'm glad we
        had that open discussion where
        we resolved all the difficulties
        caused by your brief dalliance
        with my husband, and that we are
        now all firm friends and it's all
        behind us.

                    ALEX
        Me too. Cute rabbit, by the way.

                    140

                    DAN *(Appearing at the*
                    door, and taking in the
                    tenor of the discussion)
          Hello! Glad to see you're hitting
          it off - I'll have a peppermint
          tea too, please!

Scene change #21: *A Few Good Men*

One of the most famous courtroom dramas of all time culminates in a fiery exchange between military lawyer Daniel Kaffee (Tom Cruise), and Colonel Nathan R. Jessep (Jack Nicholson). Cruise's character is attempting to exonerate a group of marines accused of murder. However, its depiction of the concept of legal 'truth' is rapidly ageing and needs to be addressed.

[INT. COURTROOM. DAY.]

KAFFEE is looking harassed. The day's
proceedings have taken their toll on
everyone. The heat is sweltering and
the fans spin lazily in the heat of the
Guantanamo Bay courthouse.

                    KAFFEE
          Do you admit that you doctored
          the logbook? That a 'Code Red'
          was sent, and that's why Private

Santiago was killed? That it's the
truth?

                JUDGE
You don't have to answer that.

                JESSEP
I'll answer it. You want answers?

                KAFFEE
I want the truth!

                JESSEP
You can't handle the truth!

                KAFFEE
What do you mean by that?

                JESSEP
Well, it's deeply subjective
and differs depending on your
perspective. Any of us might
sincerely believe very differing
things without necessarily being
wrong. Even if provably wrong by
law or so-called objective fact,
one can still believe things that
appear to differ from that. We
all have different truths, in
essence.

                    KAFFEE
That's a clear elucidation of a
rather sticky problem.

                    JESSEP
Thank you.

                    KAFFEE
However, whether I can actually
'handle' what you believe to be
the truth is not within your
purview and really is for me to
decide.

                    JESSEP
An equally persuasive argument.

                    KAFFEE
Too generous.

                    JESSEP
Not at all.

                    JUDGE
Remind me what the original
question was?

                    KAFFEE
Did you send the 'Code Red'?

JESSEP
Oh, that. Yes I did.

KAFFEE
No more questions, Your Honour!

Scene change #22: *The Silence of the Lambs*

One of the few films to win all four major Oscars (best film, best director, best actor and best actress), *Silence of the Lambs* is also one of the most effective chillers ever made. One of the nastiest lines is a casual reference by the imprisoned serial killer Hannibal Lecter (Sir Anthony Hopkins) to having eaten someone's liver with 'fava beans and a nice Chianti'. The scene is distasteful in more ways than one, as non-consensual cannibalism must not be approved of. A preferable version follows:

[INT. SECURE PSYCHIATRIC UNIT. DAY.]

It's near the end of their mutual
interrogation, and CLARICE STARLING, the
young FBI investigator, is clearly flustered
and her speech is trembling.

STARLING
You see a lot - but can you turn
that intelligence on yourself?
What would you see then?

Possibly HANNIBAL LECTER is becoming emotionally interested too. He slams shut the metal tray between them, giving her files back and making her flinch.

> LECTER
> A census taker once tried to test me. I invited him in. I made him a nice vegan mushroom risotto. We had some zero-alcohol lager and watched the footie. It's important work those census takers do.

> STARLING
> Afterwards he went missing.

> LECTER
> Yes, afterwards I murdered him because I'm a serial killer and that's my mental health journey, but I wasn't going to go into any unnecessarily gruesome details.

> STARLING
> That's very sensitive and shows that despite suffering under a serious psychiatric condition you still take into account the feelings of others.

                    LECTER
It's kind of you to point this
out. Nice perfume, by the way.

                    STARLING
Hmm. I'm going to throw a flag
on that. Complimenting a woman's
perfume is creepy.

                    LECTER
I would never want to come across
that way.

Scene change #23: *Dead Poets Society*

The film about an inspirational teacher beloved of his students can be seen through very different eyes today. The students of Robin Williams's teacher, Mr Keating, are inspired via the systematic breaking of important rules which have evolved through centuries of pedagogical experience for their safety and benefit.

For a film which seeks to embrace and give voice to the purity and fragility of the human spirit to openly encourage unsafe practices shows that it is a hypocritical and flawed work, despite its perverse popularity. A particularly famous and egregious example is the scene where the impassioned students clamber on their desks to protest the teacher's leaving. An improved and emended version follows:

[INT. CLASSROOM. DAY.]

The HEADMASTER, rather a stiff-looking
fellow, begs the students to open their
books.

> HEADMASTER
>
> Open to page 176 please. And you,
> Jenkins, start to read.

> JENKINS
>
> I can't, sir. I don't have
> that page.

> HEADMASTER
>
> Someone else, then - you've all
> got your student editions. So
> read it.

> JENKINS
>
> None of us has it. We tore it
> out, sir. Mr Keating told us to.

As the HEADMASTER stares at him in
disbelief, the door opens and MR KEATING
is standing there. The students are all
electrified by his appearance. JENKINS gets
up at once and climbs on his desk.

> JENKINS
>
> Oh Captain, my Captain!

HEADMASTER
Stop that at once! If you don't
stop, you are out of this school!

One by one, the other students follow suit.
They all climb on their desks and repeat the
mantra.

STUDENTS
Oh Captain, my Captain!

KEATING
If you would please climb down
from your desktops. It's extremely
dangerous for you to stand up
there. If you fell you could
cause injury which might have
lifelong consequences, which
would be yet another mark against
me for my many irresponsible
behaviours.

The students do so.

KEATING
Thank you. You should be aware
that many of my teaching
methods were decidedly risky and
inappropriate. Indeed, I have
quite correctly resigned and
repent my former idiosyncratic

habits, even if they did inspire
a minority of pupils.

           STUDENTS
We understand your position, Mr
Keating; it's a sensible reaction
in the circumstances.

           KEATING
I have also paid for new copies
of the student edition, which are
here for you. *(Holds out box of
books)* I apologise for impeding
your education like this and will
mend my ways.

           STUDENTS
Good luck getting another job!

           KEATING
Thanks, I'll need it.

Scene change #24: *Gone with the Wind*

The highest-grossing movie of all time for more than five
decades after its release, *Gone with the Wind* exhibits many
inappropriate attitudes which have thankfully been addressed
in trigger warnings in the current editions, especially towards
slavery and Civil-War-era Deep South America. However,
the famous final exchange between Scarlett O'Hara and

Rhett Butler, involving a man callously refusing to engage with his partner's emotional distress after they've lost a child (and saying that he 'frankly' doesn't 'give a damn'), probably needs to be rewritten. Here is a preferable treatment of the same issues:

[INT. HOUSE. DAY.]

RHETT BUTLER strides to the front door and opens it, preparing to exit. SCARLETT tries to stop him.

                  SCARLETT
        But what will I do? Where
        will I go?

                  RHETT
        Frankly, my dear, people often
        disagree about such things. I'm
        afraid I don't have a solution for
        you right now and cannot help.
        I also personally disagree with
        you about your many past actions,
        which you appear to think were
        acceptable but I consider very
        naughty at best.

                  SCARLETT
        I'm hearing you.

                    RHETT

Perhaps we may in time discuss
this again and learn to agree
with each other. But right now, I
need a minute.

                    SCARLETT

You've been honest with me and
I respect that. We all have our
separate paths to explore in
life, after all.

                    RHETT

I appreciate you.

                    SCARLETT

I appreciate you.

                    RHETT

So long then. I'll biff off into
that rather gorgeous sunset.

                    SCARLETT

Smell you later.

Scene change #25: *Star Wars Episode V: The Empire Strikes Back*

The famous ending of the *Star Wars* sequel contains one of
the great plot twists, revealing that the hero Luke Skywalker

and the villain Darth Vader are son and father respectively. What makes it unsuitable for modern audiences (and typical of the time it was made) is that the emotional issues are not dealt with but brushed under the carpet, only to resurface later, inevitably, as violent conflict. Here is a far more healthful version:

[EXT. SPACE STATION. NIGHT/DAY?]

DARTH VADER and LUKE SKYWALKER clash lightsabers. VADER is strong and LUKE falls back, clambering to safety.

> VADER
> You do not know how strong we could be together. We could rule the galaxy!

> LUKE
> I'll never join you! Obi-Wan told me what you did! You killed my father!

> VADER
> No, Luke. I *am* your father.

> LUKE
> That's not possible!

                    VADER
You've got to understand. My work
forced me to travel. I could not
look after you. I did not want
to be an absent father but I had
no choice. Possibly, in time, we
could build a relationship even
though we've missed out on those
valuable years when you were a
youngster. What do you say?

                    LUKE
It's not impossible, I guess. But
I'm not entirely pleased with your
life choices.

                    VADER
Let's take it slow! Meet up
once in a while and try to
form a bond. Possibly on one of
those swamp planets where they
have those restaurants that do
excellent salads. I've read really
good reviews . . .

                    LUKE
Me too, actually.

                    VADER
Okay, so let's, like, maybe pencil
something in?

                    153

LUKE

What's a pencil?

VADER

An ancient tool for wri . . .
It doesn't matter. I'll have my
secretary ping you with some
dates.

LUKE

I look forward to it!

VADER

Me too. Glad to get this off my
chest. Sorry for chopping your
hand off just now.

LUKE

That was certainly not ideal.

VADER

Let's talk it through.

LUKE

Let's.

VADER

Good to talk. Oh well, back to
the grindstone, I suppose.

154

Scene change #26: *Apocalypse Now*

Francis Ford Coppola's 1979 Vietnam movie is an adaptation of Joseph Conrad's masterpiece about the horrors of African colonialism, *Heart of Darkness*. One of the most upsetting scenes is where Robert Duvall's character Lieutenant Kilgore, an American military commander, boasts about the destruction his soldiers are wreaking upon the countryside, claiming, 'I love the smell of napalm in the morning.' Here is a far more palatable rendering of that scene:

[EXT. PADDY FIELD. DAY.]

CAPTAIN WILLARD is crouching in the foxhole as planes fly past.

        KILGORE
You smell that? Nothing else in
the world smells like that. I
love the smell of bánh mì in the
morning!

        WILLARD
You do?

        KILGORE
Who wouldn't? It's so fragrant.
In fact, the whole cuisine of
the Vietnamese people is magical
to me. Fresh and healthy, also
delicious!

WILLARD

I'm glad to hear you say so.
I also am invigorated by the
natural flavours and also the
beauty of the country itself.

KILGORE

I couldn't agree more. Personally,
of course, I abhor the American
military incursion into this
pastoral paradise.

WILLARD

Napalm, in particular, seems to
be exceptionally harmful and
regrettable.

KILGORE

I could not have put it
better myself. The sooner this
ghastliness ends the better.

WILLARD

You said it, Lieutenant.

Dracula
by Bram Stoker

The epistolary novel by Irish author Bram Stoker is possibly the book that gave birth to the modern horror genre. In it, solicitor Jonathan Harker travels to Romania to meet with a new client, the elderly and reclusive Count Dracula, to help him buy property in London – an early instance of wealthy foreigners buying up important housing stock in order to 'launder' their presumably ill-gotten gains.

Dracula is important, enduringly popular and deeply troubling. Although on the surface it's the Gothic tale of a supernatural monster, it is in fact clearly a far-right parable in which Eastern European immigrants are characterised as blood-sucking parasites who move to these shores in suspicious boats that arrive unexpectedly with no crew, 'take' 'our' women and spread their poison among the populace. The message is clear – Dracula is more closely related to other pestilence-spreading vermin such as bats, rats and dogs (he turns into each of these in the text) than he is to humans.

Potential trigger warnings

! Dental hygiene
! Hemophobia
! Fear of needles
! Claustrophobia – in particular, the scene in which Dracula is transported overseas in a wooden crate

Problematic quotations

'The children of the night! What music they make!': Children should certainly not be depicted staying out after dark, whether performing music (which admittedly is an admirable goal and contributes to personal development) or otherwise. They must be supervised at all times.

Suggested revisions

Dracula is an epistolary novel, and as such is confusing to modern readers – it should be written in emails, texts, Insta posts, blogs etc. It is not even necessary for Jonathan Harker to venture to Transylvania in order to have a horrific encounter with Dracula: he could just as plausibly have a Zoom or Teams meeting with him to discuss business affairs, and then discover the truth about Castle Dracula via Google reviews and a Reddit thread.

Dracula is a horrifying creature indeed – he is a wealthy elderly person with multiple rooms to spare, which he is keeping to himself in defiance of the housing shortage. He could or should be putting up refugees from other parts of Europe and the Middle East in several of the empty wings of his castle and assisting the local Romanian economy by employing a full maintenance staff instead of attempting to keep up the large property by himself.

Whether the previous point is taken or not: as a post-retirement-age person living alone, Count Dracula ought at the very least to have a visit from the council to assess if he is capable of living in the dwelling alone, and he should have weekly evaluations from a welfare officer.

Dracula travels on the merchant frigate *Demeter* to Whitby – a wholly inappropriate and nonsensical journey by today's standards, going via a sequence of transport chains that are discontinued. Recommend he ought to fly Ryanair or EasyJet, his demonic motivation inflamed by enormous punitive charges, and possibly by his wooden sarcophagus being crammed into the overhead luggage compartment.

The *Odyssey*
by Homer

The presence of the *Odyssey* as the second great literary work of Western civilisation (albeit it's really just an extension and continuation of the first, the *Iliad*) casts a sad and worrisome shadow over all other works that come after. The work glorifies its hero, the wily trickster Odysseus (or Ulysses, his Roman name), returning home ten years after the Siege of Troy.

Seen with a contemporary eye, the story is a template of self-righteous boastful toxic masculinity. Odysseus is the archetypal example of an absent father who's gone away with the lads on a violent excursion for his own gratification and self-glorification, to fight a bunch of foreigners, leaving his wife to run the home and his son to grow up fatherless.

It is an integral part of the tale (mentioned in the first line, indeed) that Odysseus is a habitual liar and manipulator: he is 'the man of twists and turns', a trickster. He arrives back from his adventures with classic tales of the swaggering male fantasist: talking of sleeping with a string of powerful, beautiful women who are uncontrollably in love with him, including a goddess and a sorceress; surviving impossible encounters with sea monsters and whirlpools, and defeating a terrifying giant cyclops. He brags about all of these over dinner to strangers on the isle of the Phaeacians. He is the ancient equivalent of the self-deluded fisherman who throws his arms wide when telling about his catch, saying, 'It was this big!'

The tone of his narration is the most suspect part: he portrays the females who imprisoned him as beautiful, but emotionally unstable and driven to insane jealousy (essentially, 'witches be crazy'). Also distasteful is his delight at having mutilated and blinded an already one-eyed person: a gleeful act of violence against the differently abled that the text heartily approves of.

In the end, Odysseus leaves behind him a string of broken homes and abusive relationships, and a trail of emotional and physical damage across the Aegean Sea – every place he visited over those ten years must groan at the thought of ever having set eyes on him.

Potential trigger warnings

! Seasickness
! Fear of horses

Problematic quotations

'Rosy-fingered dawn': the sunrise is frequently described using this formula of words, which has a suspiciously smutty edge that has titillated schoolchildren for centuries – entirely plausible when one considers the 'laddish' overall tone of the work. Replace with 'pleasant sunrise'.

'Wine-dark sea': encourages alcohol consumption, replace with 'Ribena-hued ocean'.

Suggested revisions

On his return home, Odysseus dresses as a beggar – one struggles to think of anything that could be less appropriate, seeing as he is in fact a king, which shows how out of touch he is. If disguise is necessary he ought to pose as a successful businessman selling time-share apartments on the Ithacan seafront.

Odysseus's most famous trick (of which he is characteristically boastful) is his creation of the Trojan Horse – in fact, this is a confession to a war crime and is in clear breach of the Geneva convention. At the very least, the book should conclude with his arraignment and removal to The Hague to await trial.

The text is also prejudicial towards actual Greeks bearing sincere gifts.

King Lear

by William Shakespeare

Shakespeare's tragedy about a semi-mythical English king trying to give up his kingdom and live out his final years in peace is a worrying parable for our times. Shedding his responsibilities, King Lear divides his kingdom and parcels it out between his three daughters, but behaves erratically and cannot be dealt with, frequently exploding into rage while his offspring begin to fight among themselves. Eagle-eyed readers will spot many similarities with HBO's smash hit *Succession*, which in its mercilessness and brutality is perhaps a more convincing depiction of medieval behaviour than *Lear*.

Lear himself is practically a poster child for the boomer generation – having led a comfortable and privileged life, he shifts all his responsibility on to his grown-up children and desires to continue living in comfort regardless of the financial burden.

Potential trigger warnings

! Elder abuse
! Inheritance tax avoidance
! Retirement age: Lear is attempting to retire, despite usually being played by someone in his sixties. This will be very distressing to working-age audiences who are now facing far later dates of retirement. Suggest his age is fixed at ninety-two.

Problematic quotations

'Blow, winds and crack your cheeks! rage! blow! You cataracts and hurricanoes spout': violent language some may find alarming. Suggest change to, 'Sharp westerly winds expected.'

'Nothing will come of nothing, speak again': proven to be inaccurate, as scientists have recently theorised it is possible the universe started out of nothing. Suggest change to, 'Big bang or solid-state theory, take your pick, sunshine.'

'Out, vile jelly': jelly is affordable and nutritious under current government guidelines. Suggest changing to: 'In, delicious jelly!'

'His flawed heart ... burst smilingly': clearly medically impossible, as hearts cannot smile. Suggest change to, 'He had a colossal thrombosis but did receive some good news shortly beforehand – which possibly caused it, who can tell?'

Suggested revisions

Edgar pretending to be the mentally ill character 'Poor Tom' is deeply offensive to those with serious learning difficulties. Instead, he ought to disguise himself as a mild-mannered accountant.

Even more troubling is the extremely inappropriate sequence where Edgar tricks blinded Gloucester into jumping to his death from the edge of a 'cliff', which is in fact a low wall. Instead, Edgar should put Gloucester in touch with social services to request a visit from a social worker and placement in sheltered housing.

It is entirely inappropriate to have a character referred to as the 'Fool'. He should be given a name, and it should be stated that he has just returned from a prestigious Parisian clown college.

Sense and Sensibility
by Jane Austen

Jane Austen's first published novel reaffirms myriad outdated notions of heteronormative romantic ideals. It is the first instance of her harmful and reactive worldview that has held so much sway over readers in succeeding generations. It is evident from the first that Austen had misgivings about her own recherché views – not even giving her own name to the first edition, only signing it 'A Lady'.

Suggested revisions

Austen's style has a pervasive use of irony, which is not appropriate in today's society, where all statements are always taken at face value. Suggest rewriting using ChatGPT to make the book easier to understand and more 'honest'.

In the scene where Marianne Dashwood meets Mr Willoughby, she is caught in the rain and runs down a Devonshire hill, where she slips and hurts her ankle. For safety she should be wearing a hi-vis jacket with running shorts and shoes. Equally, Mr Willoughby ought not to pick her up and carry her home, but secure the site of the accident, write a detailed incident report and call an apothecary.

Pride and Prejudice
by Jane Austen

The most famous and beloved novel by perhaps England's favourite novelist, *Pride and Prejudice* is the tale of the journey towards matrimony of Elizabeth Bennet and the proud Mr Darcy. However, this must be no excuse for the manifold errors of judgement it contains.

Problematic quotations

'It is a truth universally acknowledged . . .': one of the most famous first lines in literature has unfortunately not aged well. Surely no one can truly believe in this polarised age that there is any single fact agreed upon by all parties? The sentence goes on to insist that a man always wants a wife, a shocking or laughable conceit even taking into consideration Austen's masterful (or should that be mistresslike) command of irony. A far more palatable and comprehensible first line would be: 'No one really knows anything, except that most males are dtf.'

Title: 'pride' is a word which is undoubtedly progressive and to be encouraged but 'prejudice' is deeply harmful and one of the most profound challenges the world continues to face. Title should be changed to *Pride and Being Respectful of People's Differences*.

Suggested revisions

The Bennet family consists of five daughters, which is an irresponsible number of children in a world with diminishing resources. Evidence suggests that affluent parents are having fewer and fewer children, if any at all, so this does not reflect reality. Reduce the number of daughters to two.

Middlemarch
by George Eliot

Potential trigger warnings

SAD: title could be distressing to people with seasonal affective disorder, for whom the long winter months are the most difficult time and cause episodes of depressive mood. Change title to *Late April*.

Postman Pat
(Woodland Animations)

Postman Pat presents a vision of healthy, happy, cooperative and smooth-running small-town life. This is fundamentally inaccurate and dishonest and risks a rude awakening for youngsters, leaving them unable to function in a distrustful and rapidly deteriorating world.

It is essential that, to prevent this, the show be altered to reflect reality.

Potential trigger warnings

Cat allergies: the presence of Pat's black-and-white cat could trigger psychosomatic symptoms in sensitive viewers. Should be replaced by a hypoallergenic breed of dog such as a shih-tzu, bichon frisé or miniature schnauzer.

Problematic quotations

'Early in the morning,/just as day is dawning ...' This opening lyric could not be less accurate in reporting when post is delivered in 2024 Britain, where we are lucky to get two desultory deliveries per week, usually around teatime. Change to: 'Once in a while but who knows when/Pat will make his delivery again.'

Suggested revisions

It's true new characters with different ethnic backgrounds have been introduced to the series. However, it could go much further in striving for verisimilitude. Half the shops in Greendale High Street should be standing empty. There ought to be a marked homelessness problem, and when requested for spare change Pat should explain to rough sleepers about outreach charities which help people find secure accommodation and get back on their feet.

As the series is set on the border of North Yorkshire and Cumbria, to be strictly accurate the weather ought to be lashing rain 75 per cent of the time and there should be a rising problem of depression and suicide among the local farmers, although whether this is appropriate for a children's television programme is open to debate.

Following the Post Office scandal, public faith in the organisation is at an all-time low. In solidarity with the unfairly convicted sub-postmasters, Pat should change employer to DHL, or in fact be trying to overturn his conviction from within HMP Greendale.

Film History:
The Sensitivity Read V

Many of the most famous scenes from film history, when watched back, still have a great deal of power – to upset, that is, owing to how poorly they've dated. Here are some sensible initial attempts to sanitise the worst offenders and de-fang the most triggering moments so that we can still enjoy these masterpieces safely.

Scene change #27: *Jerry Maguire*

Cameron Crowe's 1996 film contains some of the most quotable scenes in cinema history. Tom Cruise plays the titular sports agent who – going out on his own – must persuade a major baseball star to stay signed with him. However, the message of the scene – with its repeated jubilant line, 'Show me the money!' – celebrates extreme capitalism at its worst and sets a bad example. A preferable version of this scene would run like this:

[INT. KITCHEN. DAY.]

ROD TIDWELL is shirtless in his kitchen, dancing to music on the radio and on the phone to his agent, JERRY MAGUIRE.

>   TIDWELL
> There's one thing you've got to
> do if you want to stay my agent,
> Jerry. You want to know what it
> is? Show me the money. Say it
> with me, Jerry!

>   MAGUIRE
> Show you the money?

>   TIDWELL
> Louder!

[INT. OFFICE. DAY.]

JERRY is sitting in a respectable uptown LA office, visible to multiple colleagues through glass office walls. He is decidedly embarrassed.

>   MAGUIRE *(awkward, looking
>   round)*
> Show you the money!

TIDWELL

No - it's not 'show you the money' it's 'show me the money'! Shout it!

MAGUIRE

Actually, Rod, the relentless pursuit of wealth ahead of all other things in life makes for an unsatisfactory existence.

TIDWELL

You don't say?

MAGUIRE

Yes. You're already in the upper few percentiles of a highly remunerated sector. Focus on things that bring you contentment and peace - fulfilment, satisfaction. People who desire nothing but money in life tend to end up lonely, paranoid, depressed and with a distorted sense of values. Rich as well, mostly - but rich in the least meaningful way of all.

TIDWELL

This is good advice. You are my representative not just in the

boardroom but also in matters
of the spirit! I'm going to quit
today and open a wellness retreat
for injured woodland creatures,
which has been my dream since I
was a boy!

                MAGUIRE
Yeah, okay, but you're still under
contract to the Arizona Cardinals
for two years.

                TIDWELL
I'm hanging up now to pursue my
dreams like you told me!

                MAGUIRE
    (Gulps)

Rest of film covers Maguire's attempt to free
Tidwell from contract.

Scene change #28: *Chinatown*

Roman Polanski's 1974 revisionist detective noir masterpiece
(from the Oscar-winning script by Robert Towne) has one
of the most famous final lines in history. The villain Noah
Cross (played by legendary director John Huston) has the
police shoot his own daughter Evelyn (Faye Dunaway), who
was trying to escape him to go to Mexico. As he watches,

horrified, the detective Jake Gittes (Jack Nicholson) is told: 'Forget it, Jake – it's Chinatown.' This is supposed to mean that Chinatown is a place of danger, differing morals and lowered value of human life, where the ordinary rules do not apply. It is a very clear example of 'othering'. A more progressive version would be considerably less offensive:

[EXT. LOS ANGELES CHINATOWN. NIGHT.]

A car horn rings out across the night.

NOAH CROSS reaches the car which has just crashed and grabs his screaming granddaughter from the passenger seat. He smothers her screams with his wrinkled hands as she tries to get away.

JAKE GITTES stares open mouthed at the blood on the driver's seat. It's EVELYN's blood.

One of CROSS's goons moves her body so that the horn stops. Then he faces up to GITTES.

> GOON
> Go home, Jake. I'm doing you a
> favour here. Go home!

Two police detectives take JAKE by the arms to usher him away.

                    DETECTIVE
Forget it, Jake. It's Chinatown.

                    JAKE
With its wonderful array of
delicious restaurants, you mean?

                    DETECTIVE
That's right. You're shaken up –
maybe let's get a bite to eat.

                    JAKE
Of course it isn't just Chinese
food one finds there.

                    DETECTIVE
You're right there. Korean,
Japanese, Taiwanese, Indonesian –
and others, too. I personally
fancy some soup dumplings – xiao
long bao. Delicious!

                    JAKE
It's so colourful and delightfully
decorated without being in any
way alienating or fearful. I
could really go for a bubble
tea rn.

                    DETECTIVE
          We could also go shopping for
          some ingredients to cook at home.

                      JAKE
          A fine idea. Lead on!

Scene change #29: *Airplane!*

One of the greatest comedies of the 1980s, *Airplane!* spawned
a sequel and gave lift-off to the comedy career of Leslie
Nielsen, who until then had only ever played 'straight-man'
roles (itself a phrase badly in need of updating). One particular running gag, however, has dated extremely poorly, which
is where Nielsen (as the sole doctor on board the doomed
aeroplane) repeatedly misunderstands people saying the word
'surely' for 'Shirley'. Saying that a man being called Shirley
was hilarious (which the film does over and again) is a very
bad look in 2024 and a revised, more sensitive version would
read something like this:

[INT. PLANE COCKPIT. DAY.]

The extremely nervous ex-army pilot TED
STRIKER enters the cockpit, where he's been
asked to go by a cabin attendant. He enters
to see neither pilot nor co-pilot in their
seats.

Near by is DR RUMACK, who has been seeing to
the ill pilots.

> STRIKER
> Both pilots are sick!?

> RUMACK
> Can you fly this plane?

> STRIKER
> Surely you can't be serious?

> RUMACK
> I am serious. And although it's
> entirely plausible for a man (or
> someone who appears to present
> as a cis-male, or indeed anyone
> at all, to be called Shirley or
> indeed anything he or they want,
> as it happens my name is not
> Shirley.

> STRIKER
> As a matter of fact, I was saying
> the word 'surely' spelled S, U,
> R, E, L, Y. But perhaps I should
> be careful of my diction so that
> misunderstandings like this don't
> arise in future.

RUMACK

Well, it seems that it was my
mistake. In fact, Shirley is not
that uncommon as a man's name,
irrespective of sensitivity
towards the complex issue of
gender. In 1935 it was the 259th
most common boy's name for babies
in the United States.

STRIKER

Makes you think. Certainly
nothing to chuckle about.

RUMACK

Indeed. Anyhoo, let's get on with
landing this aircraft, shall
we not?

STRIKER

More pressing matters do indeed
attend us.

Scene change #30: *The Godfather*

One of the most effective and horrifying moments in Francis
Ford Coppola's *The Godfather* (1972) comes after Don
Corleone assures his godson that he will make Jack Woltz 'an
offer he can't refuse'. Woltz is a Hollywood executive and also
the proud owner of a prize racehorse whose head is cut off and

left in Woltz's bed as a warning. It is a scene that is distressing for animal lovers and owners of horses, not to mention horse fetishists and laundry workers who have to try to eradicate especially stubborn and unpleasant stains. It should be changed to something less traumatic, such as what follows:

[INT. HOLLYWOOD MANSION. NIGHT.]

JACK WOLTZ is asleep in bed, covered by silk sheets. He stirs in his sleep. Stirs again – then wakes up and throws back the sheets.

He screams.

His WIFE appears in the doorway, putting on some face cream.

        WIFE
What is it, Jack?

        WOLTZ
I just remembered I forgot to
reply to that nice Mr Corleone
accepting his generous offer!
I *must* remember to do that
tomorrow!

        WIFE
I know how you hate to be
discourteous in such affairs.

```
            Don't forget. He seems a nice
            enough man to do business with.

                      WOLTZ
            That's true. Undoubtedly a tough
            negotiator, but I respect that.
            Now, time for beddy-byes; I don't
            want to be tired for the big race
            meeting tomorrow.

                      WIFE
            Very sensible, darling. It's a
            big day!

                      WOLTZ  (hopping back
                      into bed)
            Night night!
```

Scene change #31: *Mrs Doubtfire*

The 1993 comedy hit *Mrs Doubtfire*, in which Robin Williams plays a down-on-his-luck actor who impersonates an elderly Scottish nanny in order to gain access to his own children, is the epitome of a movie about which people say 'it could not be made today'. To render it at all palatable to contemporary viewers, the film would have to be cut down to about fifteen minutes, with something like this as the concluding scene:

[INT. WORKSHOP. DAY.]

Recently divorced actor DANIEL HILLARD has just lost custody of his kids. In desperation he visits his brother FRANK, a make-up specialist, to ask for help.

DANIEL knocks on the door. It swings open – his brother stands there.

> FRANK
>
> Daniel!

> DANIEL
>
> Can you make me a woman?

> FRANK
>
> Honey, come in!

They enter.

> FRANK
>
> Explain to me why you want to do this.

> DANIEL
>
> I've lost custody of the kids. So I want to dress up as a Scottish nanny and fake a résumé so I can infiltra—

                    FRANK
Wait, wait - stop talking. You're
making me an accessory to a
felony at this point. Answer me
this: do you have a compulsion to
wear feminine clothing?

                    DANIEL
In this instance, yes, very much.

                    FRANK
Daniel, answer me honestly.

                    DANIEL
Well . . . no.

                    FRANK
So for you to do so is actually
insulting to those who *do*
feel that compulsion, do you
understand? In fact (whether you
mean it that way or not), you are
mocking their way of life.

                    DANIEL
Sure, I see that. But the kids—

                    FRANK
You've lost custody because
you are unreliable and act
unpredictably, instead of giving

                    185

those children the stability they
desperately need. Capisce?

          DANIEL
Yes.

          FRANK
Enabling you to pull a stunt
like this - which is inevitably
going to go wrong - will likely
harm them and you even further.
You need to grow up. Get steady
work - teach alongside your
acting. Perhaps get some therapy.
Show your ex-wife you can be a
sensible and stable person. In
time she will be delighted to
give you back custody.

          DANIEL
Wow. Shit. I'm pretty lucky
you gave me this talking-to
right now.

          FRANK
You certainly are. Now off
you go, and no more insane
transphobic stunts and bad
Scottish accents, do you hear?

DANIEL
I'm lucky to have you as a
brother.

[END CREDITS]

Shipping Forecast
(BBC Radio 4)

The *Shipping Forecast* was once an essential tool to protect seafaring vessels against extremely dangerous changeable conditions, enabling them to continue their work which was so crucial to international trade. It was rendered technologically irrelevant by the early 2000s but instead of being removed from the airwaves to make way for something with genuine utility, it was 'saved' by an emotional listener campaign.

In so doing it was transformed from an essential life-saving communication tool to a redundant upper-middle-class comfort blanket, a kind of ASMR Mogadon-by-John Lewis, and therefore a mockery and insult towards its original purpose.

The people who are so fixated upon this peculiar piece of smooth-voiced nonsense poetry are those of the educated classes and higher income brackets – the gatekeepers and preservers of the status quo. The very people who apparently consider themselves decent and liberal-minded, but whose stubborn inaction and silent microaggressions ensure that true systemic change always seems possible but never arrives. It is these listeners who literally use the *Shipping Forecast* to help them sleep at night.

Thus behind the *Shipping Forecast*'s syllabic contortions (meaningless yet mystical; calm and Anglophone and always in received pronunciation) it has some kind of talismanic force, and it pulses into the sleeping brains of the comfortable and pampered, like a reassuring beacon, signifying the permanent tidal ebb and flow of unfair systems of repression, so that they can awake soothed and carry on as though nothing is really wrong.

Switching off this programme would help us all to wake up and protect everyone (not just those at sea) from the prevailing gale-force winds.

Problematic language

Many areas mentioned within the forecast have outdated names which should be altered to reflect modern society:

Viking, Trafalgar: a needless echo of the aggressive militaristic past, should be replaced with peaceful terms such as Soft Play and Quiet Carriage.

Boulmer: often pronounced 'boomer'; it is typical of the superior treatment that boomers receive in every way that they should get a specific 'shout out' on their beloved broadcast. Change to 'Gen Z'.

Fastnet: an internet service provider based in Brighton should not receive twice-daily free advertising on the BBC

Dogger: inappropriate.

German Bight: sounds violent, alter to 'German Respectful Disagreement'.

'Good', 'moderate' and 'poor' are tepid, old-fashioned terms; change to 'sick', 'cba' and 'basic'.

Planet Earth
(BBC One)

One cannot but be impressed by the almighty chutzpah of the BBC in presenting to gullible viewers such a farrago of invention and fiction as the documentaries of David Attenborough and pretending that they are 'non-fiction'. Indeed, it shows the egregiously outdated paternalistic attitude of the BBC itself, not only in retaining Attenborough's patrician and elitist tones but in presenting its meticulously crafted and manipulated narratives as though they are a realistic depiction of the natural world. These shows are more obviously examples of 'structured reality' than *The Only Way is Essex* and *Made in Chelsea*.

First there is the frankly deceitful nature of the extremely carefully edited footage, then there is the far worse fictive layer in the anthropomorphism of the sleepy voiceover in which human emotions are inappropriately attributed to animals. The final insult might be the fact that in recent series, all the animal 'stories' presented in bite-sized ten-minute chunks (emblematic again of pandering to the supposedly attention-deficit Snapchat generation as though they are incapable of handling any form of complexity) – *none* of them contain death. Endangered animals always escape. Nature here is not red in tooth and claw but relaxing in a comfy jumper and filing its nails!

For the programme to reflect in any way the supposed honesty and transparency of the BBC's much vaunted public service brief, the footage should be presented raw, with no music or voiceover, just dozens of hours of silence and stillness broken only by brief flurries of activity, with death presented in all its violent frankness.

A contextual explanatory intro/outro would be presented *not* by an Oxbridge-educated 'national treasure' born during the reign of George V, but someone youthful and vibrant to connect with 'ordinary' people (George Ezra or Vernon Kay, for instance). The closing music would be a track of urban beats.

University Challenge
(BBC Two)

The fact that this perennial favourite quiz show has been a hit with audiences ever since it was first broadcast in 1962 shows why it must be time to replace it with something new. The 'venerable' nature of many old shows often prevents (or delays) their being regarded through a suitably analytical lens, which all *new* programmes naturally receive. Therefore, let's see what we have in front of us and whether we feel it ought to be allowed to continue.

Here is a format unashamedly aimed at elitist university-educated audiences, where a Cambridge-educated man demands answers and openly castigates and mocks participants' wrong responses, often yelling at them to hurry up. This bullying and abusive power structure is out of date with contemporary university experience: in fact, students these days are 'customers' with a lot of power of approval and review over the courses they are paying for. A more accurate quiz show would be one in which the participants quiz the chair over his credentials and right to question them in the first place.

Equally, the spirit of competitive one-upmanship is not appropriate to foster an atmosphere of learning and co-operation. Instead, the show should encourage individuals to explore their own individual paths and report back with their findings to share with the group in a supportive environment.

It's known that many of the most intelligent and valuable members of society are not university educated, just as much as it's acknowledged that some of the worst scoundrels who've disgraced the field of public life have the 'best' educations in the land. Therefore, why restrict the teams in such a way – include groups from any field of life, such as dairy or slaughterhouse workers, jobseekers, prisoners or children.

It would not have to always be a quiz but could alternate other activities such as contestants pushing each other off a spinning pole into a pit of brightly coloured gunge, playing dodgeball, or jointly icing a cake – although it would be best if there is no score system and no winners are announced.

Hey Duggee
(Studio AKA)

Another apparently innocent and charming animation which entertains children and adults alike, *Hey Duggee* hides its harmful ingredients in plain sight.

It is a show for primary-school-age children in which a group of youngsters solve a problem by applying and learning a certain kind of skill – for which they are awarded a scouting badge. This is emblematic of the feeble 'everyone gets a prize' approach to life that has weakened British mental resilience and competitiveness on the world stage, debilitating children while it patronises them, and reducing the value of genuine achievements.

Then, of course, there is the fact that the programme is – from first frame to last – an uncritical endorsement of and advertisement for the Scout Movement, an elderly and deeply problematic organisation with its basis in some decidedly peculiar attitudes to youth in the early twentieth century, and a shining beacon for sex offenders across the decades.

Add to this the fact that the Scout Master and title

character, Duggee, can only say one word: 'woof!' This is a term used to express arousal by men of a certain generation, a way of laughing off or excusing unwanted advances. And how does each episode end? With this frankly dubious hound *demanding a hug*. With these facts looked at soberly, it seems impossible that it can remain on the airwaves.

Charlotte's Web
by E. B. White

In print ever since its first publication in 1952, the beloved classic of American children's literature is about a baby pig growing up on a farm who does not know he's destined for the slaughter – and the female spider who takes pity on him and decides to save his life by spinning a series of webs containing messages that astound the farm's human owners. The book's enduring appeal is in its simple and charming message of love – which is unfortunately out of date.

It is yet another of the numerous works in literature which show how a female's hard work is used only to credit a lazy male. Looking upon webs that describe the pig as 'radiant' and 'humble', so inherent is the misogyny of the humans that they are unable to ascribe these feats to any female power and automatically heap glory upon the porcine male (who it is perfectly obvious is physically unable to spin a web).

Suggested revisions

Indeed, having composed the webs, Charlotte dies of exhaustion without a shred of recognition. This section's truthfulness has sadly not diminished in the many decades since its publication and ought possibly to be augmented to make things *even worse*, where after her death Wilbur angrily denies anyone but himself was responsible for the webs until he is exposed and shamed, long afterwards, by Charlotte's arachnid offspring.

One element which must be altered is the depiction of an American farm as a peaceful and harmonious bucolic idyll – to be accurate, this should be depicted as a hotbed of Trumpian truth-denial (which would chime with Wilbur's rewriting of history) and insurrectionist fervour. In this version the barn should probably be changed to an apocalyptic 'prepper' bunker filled with canned goods, guns and bibles.

Moby-Dick
by Herman Melville

Although a disappointment on its first publication and out of print at its author's death in 1891, *Moby-Dick*, the tale of the fatal obsession of Captain Ahab with the infamous white whale, has come to be seen as a masterpiece of world literature, its profile boosted by the admiration shown by William Faulkner and D. H. Lawrence among other early twentieth-century authors.

It was criticised on publication by British reviewers because it seemed to be from the first-person perspective of a narrator who is killed in the final scene – this was because the book's British publisher had censored certain parts of the novel before publication, including the afterword which described the rescue of the narrator, Ishmael.

However, changing attitudes have revealed some unsavoury elements which indicate to us that perhaps the censor's pen has not finished with the work yet.

Problematic language

Character name: Starbuck – inappropriate product placement; it also encourages caffeine consumption, which is deleterious to public heart- and brain-health.

Suggested revisions

It is an all-male affair, which must be frowned upon, with no single female even glimpsed in the book's enormous 800-page span. Half the crew of the boat ought to be turned into females. Or the whale should be made female, so that it is her dominant strength that in the end destroys the males despite their stalkerish obsession with her. (In which case the name Moby-Dick would not be appropriate and Moby-Vagina would be better.)

It is regrettable that in his obsessive loathing for the whale, Captain Ahab's mental health journey is not brought to a beneficial conclusion. In an alternative ending to the book he could share his feelings with his crew and learn to grow, and perhaps at the end set up a whale sanctuary.

The white whale: equating the colour white with evil might be considered perfectly reasonable by some readers but equally be emotionally damaging to others, especially sufferers from albinism; suggest change to yellow or some other colour, or remove reference to colour at all and just call it the 'big whale'.

The book's obsession with *sperm* whales and description of the recovery of thousands of gallons of slimy pearlescent spermaceti from the whales' skulls might be triggering for some readers. It also promotes and excuses the oil trade. Suggest that financial purpose of the boat's journey be changed to transporting 'green' smokeless fuels.

The whale-slaughtering scenes are detailed, intense and grisly: very upsetting for animal lovers and whale conservationists. Replace these with a sequence of friendly and nurturing events, where the sailors are depicted coming alongside a whale and mending a cut on its back with a plaster or giving it a pretty jumper that they have all knitted together.

To chime with contemporary audiences, a better alternative version would have the titular animal not a whale but a catfish, and that Ahab is responding to emotional hurt at having been misled by a dating scenario, albeit one conducted via the pages of the *Whaler's Gazetteer* rather than on Tinder. (Although Whalr would be a compromise – an app for people searching for plus-size partners in the merchant navy.)

Bluey
(Ludo Studio)

Rarely has a TV programme been welcomed with open arms across all sections of society as has the Australian children's show *Bluey* (ages 4+); it is widely regarded as warm-hearted and inclusive to a T. However, it is exactly such programmes that warrant close attention, and even here it is quickly apparent that a grievous and subversive influence is at play.

Problematic character names

Although the messaging is on point, run a sceptical eye down the list of character names and they pop out at you. Once you see it, you cannot un-see it.

BLUEY: 'bluey' has commonly been used as a term for various drugs, as a sort of abbreviation/nickname for 'blue pill'. Usually in the UK it refers to a 'downer' containing diazepam (or other benzodiazepines) mixed with various controlled substances. It is also a slang term for Viagra, and in America is a street name for the opioid oxycodone. It is unthinkable the purveyors of this supposedly safe show for impressionable children don't know this and are not laughing behind our backs. But perhaps that's the purpose: after all, it has become popular among conspiracy theorists to refer to the choice between the 'red pill' (which wakens people up to the horrific reality) and the 'blue pill' or 'bluey' (which keeps people sedated and in a condition of blissful ignorance). The message of the show's name is clear.

BINGO (Bluey's little sister): bingo is gambling, a habit-forming behaviour which is inappropriate to advertise to minors, and the wide-eyed and innocent Bingo typifies the sort of person most likely to get pulled into a harmful and addictive cycle which can ruin lives.

BANDIT (Bluey's father): a bandit is a robber, a roadside thief, ambusher, cutpurse, an opportunistic and violent criminal. There is no positive definition of it. Why present a caring and loving father with such a name? In fact, bandits are well known to be absent fathers and have little sense of parental responsibility, which gives the young audience a false expectation of real life.

CHILLI (Bluey's mother): a delicious food for adults, but certainly not for small children! Also, she works as a security officer at the airport. One might reasonably take a very hard look at writers (who know so much about street drug terminology) who appear to have such a close interest in the workings of airport security.

Other troubling character names abound, but a few are BRANDY (Bluey's aunt), a strong intoxicating liquor;

FRISKY (Bluey's godmother), which is not a concept necessary to explore at all in such a forum, and SNICKERS (Bluey's friend), which is an unhealthy salty, sugar-filled, highly calorific product (and brand name) that ought not to be advertised to unsuspecting children.

The Indiana Jones films
(1981, 1984, 1989, 2008, 2023)

No one currently thinks it is acceptable for a piece of entertainment to depict a white man rushing around the world gathering up cultural artefacts from other civilisations. Nevertheless, those aren't the only grounds on which Indiana Jones makes for decidedly uncomfortable viewing in 2024.

Potential trigger warnings

! Lack of seatbelt when driving at speed
! Triggering for those with fear of rope bridges and sufferers of vertigo
! Complete lack of respect for road safety
! Fear of whips

Problematic quotations

'It belongs in a museum!': should instead be said of Dr Jones.

'Snakes – why did it have to be snakes?': snakes are an essential part of the ecosystem in which they live, and most are perfectly safe. They should not be stigmatised or made unreasoning objects of fear.

Suggested revisions

The caves in which Dr Jones finds himself are often swarming and seething with insects, which are depicted as monstrous and revolting. Insects offer valuable sources of protein and are likely to be essential to the food security of mankind in the future. Insert a scene where he pops one in his mouth and comments on how delicious it is. Alternatively, the insects (as things to be feared) ought to be digitally replaced by non-recyclable plastic trash and broken climate change agreements from multiple G8 summits.

The lengthy chase in *The Temple of Doom* takes place within a coal mine – this is outdated technology and ought to be changed to take place at a wind farm.

Blue Peter
(BBC One)

A flagship programme in more ways than one, *Blue Peter* is in dire need of attention thanks to its troubled history and deeply problematic content. The title alone, which is the name of a flag and the sea shanty musical accompaniment, are references to the harsh and brutal maritime life of the Royal Navy, with its reliance on alcohol rations, brutal public lashings, ill treatment of cabin boys, serious danger of death and inappropriate utilisation of biscuits.

The patriarchal tone of *Blue Peter* has an elitist edge which makes many viewers uncomfortable, and with its patronising virtue-signalling over recycling (some would say green-washing) it doesn't prepare young viewers for life in a consumerist society.

Potential trigger warnings

! Hornpipe

! Animal dung
! Sticky-back plastic

Problematic quotations

'Here's one I made earlier': redolent of the easy 'quick-fix' mentality that is so harmful to young people.

Suggested revisions

The *Blue Peter* garden, which is nurtured and tended by hosts and guests alike, has famously been vandalised on more than one occasion. Vandalism is a leisure activity for many viewers and to engage with this section of the audience, the garden should be vandalised on a weekly basis but in new and interesting ways to foster creativity.

In its friendly advice, clean bright studio and determinedly cheerful demeanour, *Blue Peter* deliberately refuses to reflect society and the lived experience of its viewership – thereby lying to children. To be strictly truthful and honest, it ought to be filmed in a Wetherspoons pub, and feature adult hosts who are entirely distracted and on their phones while children are largely left to fend for themselves.

In the early 2000s *Blue Peter* was notoriously embroiled in a scandal over the naming of a pet kitten, where executives deliberately rigged a democratic vote. In this respect alone, *Blue Peter* was ahead of its time and should regularly feature rigged elections in order to prepare children for adult life.

Toy Story
(1995, dir. John Lasseter)

The beloved film franchise has had four films and shows no sign of stopping, with a fifth entry in the works. But that doesn't mean that we ought not to cast a stern glance over certain aspects of the original film. Nearly all the toys that feature in this supposedly 'family friendly' movie have serious question marks over them, as detailed below.

Potential trigger warnings

! Choking hazards
! Deliberately burned and mutilated toys

Problematic quotations

'To infinity and beyond!': to go beyond infinity is impossible and fosters an illogical and unmathematically precise notion of the universal laws of physics. Change to: 'Let's go!'

Suggested revisions

It is inaccurate to depict dinosaurs and cowboys living alongside each other, and encourages ahistorical views; the dinosaur character ought to be changed to a giraffe.

Mr Potato Head's inclusion is a tacit approval of a carbohydrate-heavy diet, which can lead to obesity and heart disease. Suggest he is changed to Mr Tofurkey Head.

The soldier characters all appear to be male and of the same colour (green). The army should be altered to reflect the modern diverse characteristic of the armed forces, encompassing different genders and ethnicities. To reflect the mental health challenges faced by real-life veterans, it would be wise to portray some of the characters suffering with PTSD and other combat-related syndromes.

The name 'Woody' is inappropriate. Change to Woodrow or something more contemporary like Kyle.

Although Woody wears a sheriff's badge, we never see any evidence of an election – some should be added – and Woody's laid-back approach to life gives an inaccurate impression of the detailed administrative duties a modern sheriff faces, such as balancing the Police Department budget. Add a scene where he has to make difficult cuts to services owing to fiscal shortfall.

Hamm, the piggy bank, is non-vegetarian, non-vegan, non-kosher and unsuitable for vast swathes of the audience. It is not at all clear why banks ought to be pigs in the first place – the implication seems to be that by saving money, over time one will fill its belly and make the pig fatter while your savings swell. This attitude is derogatory towards pigs and should be suppressed. Suggest this toy character is just a talking bank building.

Bo Peep's traditional shepherdess costume (unless she is supposed to be going to a fancy-dress party) is inappropriate. She ought accurately to reflect the dress of a modern sheep farmer: coarse woollen jumper, baggy trousers and wellington boots, all liberally splashed with mud and animal faeces. Equally, her porcelain skin sets unrealistic skincare expectations for young girls; suggest her character is remodelled using pumice instead.

The Gruffalo
by Julia Donaldson

The bestselling *Gruffalo* is a popular hit, with sales figures as grotesquely monstrous as the titular creature. However, if we look closely there are strange undercurrents at play in the work, in which a mouse instinctively lies to everyone he meets and puts his own values on them, leaving behind a trail of neuroses and emotional damage. Yet each time he gets away with it he faces zero repercussions. Is this the message with which we ought to be lulling children to sleep?

The mouse is far from a good role model, embodying the character traits of irresponsible online influencers and conspiracy theorists, leading his 'followers' (the owl, the fox, the snake) into believing harmful fictions, for example that the Gruffalo adores owl ice cream, scrambled snake, and so on – there is no evidence for this.

Potential trigger warnings

! Nut allergies
! Cryptozoology

Problematic quotations

'. . . the mouse looked good': each of the creatures who meet the mouse thinks that it looks good, and invites it to lunch. Yet it is the automatic assumption on the part of the mouse (and perhaps many unwitting readers) that these friendly creatures have an ulterior motive and ought to be terrorised. There is no actual evidence that any of them have anything other than the best intentions, except in the mind of the mouse.

Suggested revisions

Ideally the book would have a coda – or in fact a second half – where the mouse retraces his steps, makes amends for his rude assumptions and tries to mend bridges with those he has harmed.

The entire plot revolves around the mouse's unassuageable reliance on nuts as a foodstuff, which drives him into danger and creates mayhem. He should engage with counselling and employ a nutritionist or food trainer to manage his problem, reduce his intake and get him on to a balanced diet.

The Repair Shop
(BBC One)

This programme is a symptom of a psychologically unhealthy and backward-looking culture which clings on to the past. In it, cynical artisans take in family objects with personal histories and then for their own aggrandisement prove that they can return them to their former condition. In doing so, they ensure that these sentimental artefacts will remain yoked round the neck of the unwitting participants for years to come, arresting the process of dealing with generational trauma, and preventing them from moving on and living fulfilled lives.

The programme runs on sentiments like 'Grandad would have been so proud' – however, the absent relative in question clearly did not take sufficient care of the item themselves. This is another demonstration of the way in which the current generation shoulders the burden of the carelessness of those who went before.

Suggested revisions

It would be far better to have an opening segment where familial trinkets are thrown into a skip (or if possible recycled) and then replaced by a bracing shopping trip to Ikea or Matalan.

When artefacts are returned, the reliable weeping by the item owners does not properly reflect the emotional timbre of the modern British family. Instead, some should simply pocket the goods with a curt 'thank you' and be filmed placing them on eBay.

Gogglebox
(Channel 4)

In the age of social media, where everyone has the opportunity to speak their opinions publicly, it is egregious and inappropriate that a small handful of individuals are given an elevated platform through which to mock others' hard work. One baulks at the idea of someone who thinks that their opinions are so important they ought to be put forward as some kind of moral arbiter, to praise and castigate according to their self-important and unqualified egotistical whims.

Suggested revisions

The participants ought to read extensive show notes for each of the programmes they are criticising and interview the writers, producers etc., to understand all of the aspects that went into making it, before coming to a sound, balanced and reasoned conclusion which they present in writing and read from a statement.

The Progressive Songbook

Even though the old-fashioned stage musical is synonymous with wholesome family entertainment, many of the songs they contain are startlingly inappropriate and in need of revision. Here are a few examples of how they could be updated:

Oklahoma!

Song: '*I Cain't Say No*'

Sung by Ado Annie, who describes herself as 'a girl who cain't say no', the song was in many ways ahead of its time in addressing the female libido in a non-judgemental context. However, the song has a grey area around what it means by 'saying no' – suggest make this clearer. The opening line could be changed to: 'I'm just a girl who is sex positive but goes for regular checks at the STD clinic and always ensures I have my partner's consent and my partner waits for mine.'

Song: 'Oh What a Beautiful Morning'

The cheerful and optimistic tone of the song does not ring true today and is not a plausible sentiment for a rational sane human character. Change to: 'It's too warm if anything/ We've really got to get a handle on this climate crisis shit/ There's a mental health epidemic out there.'

West Side Story

Song: 'America'

To people outside the North American continent, the concept of actually wanting to live in America is far-fetched. Alter the tone to make a satirical song, including lyrics about rapidly decaying democracy, gun violence, lack of affordable health-care, the opioid epidemic and more.

Song: 'Gee, Officer Krupke'

A sad and alarming number about disenfranchised youths plotting how best to manipulate the American social services system by pretending to have a variety of psychiatric conditions; the song is surprisingly fresh – but the list of ailments need to be updated to include chronic stress, obesity, ADHD, ASMR and screen addiction.

Song: 'I Feel Pretty'

The song is a sudden, exuberant expression of joy. To be comprehensible by today's audience, Maria should be singing it into her phone to her followers, thanking them for subscribing and following her, and for likes and comments, and the song should possibly be called '#blessed'.

Oliver!

Song: 'Food, Glorious Food'

The contents of the meals that the young people are singing about are a nutritionist's nightmare: hot sausages, saveloys, steak, cream, custard ... This song desperately needs to be updated to comply with guidance from the UK Chief Medical Officer. Foods that should be inserted into the lyrics could include lentils, nuts, seeds, quinoa, kefir and antioxidant-rich goji berries.

Song: 'You've Got to Pick a Pocket or Two'

Although the characters are caught in a difficult societal situation and their plight is to be understood and empathised with, it is still not appropriate for a popular song to encourage highway larceny. The song should be rewritten with the young thieves encouraging each other to go back to school and learn transferable skills that will help them get ahead on the job market.

Song: 'Boy for Sale'

This is not acceptable.

My Fair Lady

Song: 'Why Can't A Woman Be More Like a Man?'

Obviously this is outdated and offensive. A preferable title
(and a perfectly reasonable question which many feel ought
to be asked) would be, 'Why Can't People Stop Asking Dumb
Questions About Gender?'

Song: 'Wouldn't It Be Loverly'

The poor homeless female urchin dreams of finding a place
to live. Considering today's housing shortages, the following
lyrics should reflect the stark reality for new homeowners: 'All
I want is a room somewhere/It'll probably have to be outside
the M25 at this rate/I'll probably be retirement age before I
can afford it, though.'

Song: 'Get Me to the Church on Time'

The sentiment of this song not only encourages disrespect
towards the important institution of marriage, it also encourages binge drinking. The lyrics ought to be altered in line
with current NHS alcohol-consumption targets and also to
give a positive example to those about to get married: 'I'm
getting married in the morning/Going to go to bed early and

get a good night's sleep/After all this is a big step and I take my responsibilities seriously.'

Song: 'The Rain in Spain'

It would be considered shocking today for a privileged person to try to teach someone of a different class background what they thought was 'proper' speech. The song is also extremely insensitive to Spaniards, owing to the shocking *lack* of rain on the Spanish plains, where drought is a serious problem not likely to go away soon. If the song must be retained, it ought to be about Eliza explaining that the notion some people's accents are 'better' than others is a grossly skewed perspective – possibly by making metaphorical reference to a renewable forest rather than barren plains.

Mary Poppins

Song: 'A Spoonful of Sugar'

Medicine ought to be taken with a glass of water and definitely not sugar. The suggestion of adding extra sugar on top of the average diet (already dangerously high in sugar) is likely only to bring about the necessity of taking further medicine. Change to: 'Medicine is good for you so take it and be grateful you have access to a free NHS (for the time being anyway).'

Song: 'Chim Chim Cher-ee'

The chimney sweep is talking about how incredibly happy he is to have his particular job. 'A sweep is as lucky as a man can be,' he sings. Like the permanent grime under the sweep's fingernails, this just won't wash. This is grotesquely inaccurate and can be seen as trying to 'whitewash' the abusive and exploitative employment practices forced on the working classes in the totally regulation-free nineteenth century. The song should be changed to reflect the extreme health deficiencies endured by chimney sweeps at the time, including black lung, no holiday pay or healthcare, psychological trauma, and social outcast status thanks to false accusations of blacking up owing to soot coverage.